Peace

THROUGH LAW

BY

HANS KELSEN

THE LAWBOOK EXCHANGE, LTD.
Clark, New Jersey
2008

ISBN-13: 978-1-58477-920-9 (paperback)
ISBN-10: 1-58477-920-9 (paperback)
ISBN-13: 978-1-58477-103-6 (cloth)
ISBN-10: 1-58477-103-8 (cloth)

THE LAWBOOK EXCHANGE, LTD.

33 Terminal Avenue
Clark, New Jersey 07066-1321

*Please see our website for a selection of our other publications
and fine facsimile reprints of classic works of legal history:*
www.lawbookexchange.com

Library of Congress Cataloging-in-Publication Data

Kelsen, Hans, 1881-1973.
    Peace through law / by Hans Kelsen.
        p. cm.
    Originally published: Chapel Hill : The University of North Carolina Press, 1944.
    Includes bibliographical references and index.
    ISBN 1-58477-103-8 (cloth : alk. paper)
        1. Pacific settlement of international disputes. 2. Arbitration, International. 3.War
crimes. 4. Peace. I. Title.

KZ6010 .K45 2000
341.7'3--dc21   00-036236

Printed in the United States of America on acid-free paper

Peace

THROUGH LAW

BY

HANS KELSEN

Chapel Hill

THE UNIVERSITY OF NORTH CAROLINA PRESS

1944

To

FRANK M. RUSSELL

ACKNOWLEDGMENT

The writer wishes to thank the *American Journal of International Law,* the *American Journal of Sociology,* the *Yale Law Journal,* the *California Law Review,* and the *Journal of Legal and Political Sociology* for permission to reprint portions of articles of his which they had previously published.

PREFACE

WHEN WE LEARN, in the history of religions, about human sacrifices offered by primitive peoples to their gods; when we read that the Incas, these relatively civilized Indians, immolated even their own children on the altars of their idols in a most cruel manner, allowing the priests to cut the breasts of the victims and to take out their hearts while yet palpitating; when we try in vain to understand how parents could themselves voluntarily bear such misery, we feel relief in the comfortable consciousness of living in an enlightened age under the blessings of a higher religion which impresses upon us the supreme duty of preserving the life of man.

But have we men of a Christian civilization really the right to relax morally? May we really consider ourselves so greatly advanced in comparison with the aborigines of Peru? Has our twentieth century not brought to mankind, together with the most prodigious achievements of technique, two world wars whose human sacrifices by far eclipse the child murder of the pagan Incas? Can we refuse to comprehend these mothérs and fathers whilst we ourselves are so proud to place the flower of our own youth on altars which differ from those of the Incas only in that no religion justifies the shedding of precious blood as a result of nothing but nationalistic folly?

There are truths which are so self-evident that they must

be proclaimed again and again in order not to be doomed to oblivion. Such a truth is: that war is mass murder, the greatest disgrace of our culture, and that to secure world peace is our foremost political task, a task much more important than the decision between democracy and autocracy, or capitalism and socialism; for there is no essential social progress possible as long as no international organization is established by which war between the nations of this earth is effectively prevented.

It would be unjust to ignore the many efforts which so far have been made by statesmen and intellectuals aiming at the idea of world peace. We must, however, admit that all these efforts have been in vain, that, in spite of them, social history, in this respect, shows regress rather than progress. This may be so because the statesmen almost always have ventured too little and the intellectuals have frequently demanded too much. The League of Nations was certainly too little; the dream of a World State is certainly too much. President Wilson's work, however, notwithstanding all its imperfection, was at least a very useful beginning, whereas a utopian pacifism is in any case a serious danger.

He who, not as an active statesman but as a simple writer, tries to fulfill his duty in the struggle for world peace is no less responsible than the former. He must, in order not to compromise the great ideal, accommodate his postulates to what is politically possible; that means, not to what was yesterday possible and, consequently, is today real—this is, Heaven knows, little enough. Nor must his scheme point toward a goal which, if at all, can be reached only in a distant future; this is unreal and therefore politically less than nothing. A conscientious writer must direct his suggestions to what, after careful examination of political reality, may be considered as being possible tomorrow, although it, per-

haps, seems not yet possible today. Otherwise there would
be no hope for progress. His scheme should involve no revolution of international relations but reform of their order
by an improvement of the social technique prevailing in
this field.

The specific technique of the order regulating the relations between States is the Law of Nations. He who wishes
to approach the aim of world peace in a realistic way must
take this problem quite soberly, as one of a slow and steady
perfection of the international legal order. This is the way
in which this book tries to contribute to the most burning
problem of our time.

Berkeley, California
June, 1944   *Hans Kelsen*

CONTENTS

Part I

xi

Contents

Part II

Annex I

Annex II

Part I

PEACE GUARANTEED BY
COMPULSORY ADJUDICATION OF
INTERNATIONAL DISPUTES

1. Peace through force or through law?

PEACE IS A STATE characterized by the absence of force. Within an organized society, however, absolute absence of force—the idea of anarchism—is not possible. The employment of force in the relationship between individuals is prevented by being reserved for the community. To guarantee peace the social order does not exclude all kinds of coercive acts; it authorizes certain individuals to perform such acts under certain conditions. The employment of force, in general forbidden as a delict, is exceptionally permitted as a reaction against the delict, that is, as a sanction. The individual who, authorized by the social order, performs coercive acts against other individuals acts as an organ of the social order or—what amounts to the same—as an agent of the community constituted by that order. Only the individual through whom the community acts, only the organ of the community, is competent to perform a coercive act as a sanction directed against the violator of the order, the delinquent. Thus the social order makes the use of force a monopoly of the community and by so doing pacifies the mutual relations of its members.

It is the essential characteristic of the law as a coercive order to establish a community monopoly of force.

In a primitive legal community, too, certain individuals only are permitted to perform coercive acts under certain

3

circumstances precisely determined by the law. It is the individual or the group whose right has been violated who is authorized to employ force against the individual or the group responsible for the violation of the law. Although in primitive law the principle of self-help prevails, the coercive act which is not considered to be a delict, such as blood revenge, for instance, has the character of a sanction and is interpreted as a reaction of the legal community against the wrongdoer and his group responsible for the delict. Insofar as self-help is' recognized as a legal principle, as its execution is conceived of as an action of the legal community and a sanction against the delinquent, it is the exercise of the community monopoly of force.

When the exercise of this monopoly is centralized, when the right of employing force as a sanction is withdrawn from the injured individuals and transferred to a central agency, when a centralized executive power comes into existence, the legal community becomes a State.

The modern State is the most perfect type of a social order establishing a community monopoly of force. Its perfection is due to the centralization of the employment of force (which must not be confused with its monopolization). Within the State, pacification of inter-individual relations—that is, *national* peace—is attained in the highest possible degree. Except under certain extraordinary circumstances, such as revolution or civil war, the employment of force is effectively eliminated from relations between citizens and reserved for central agencies, as governments and courts, that are authorized to use force as sanctions against illegal acts.

When the question arises how to secure *international* peace, how to eliminate the most terrible employment of force—namely, war—from inter-State relations, no answer seems to be more self-evident than this: to unite all individual States or, at least, as many as possible, into a World State, to concentrate all their means of power, their armed forces, and put them at the disposal of a world government under laws created by a world parliament. If States are allowed to continue their existence only as members of a powerful world federation, then peace among them will be secured as effectively as among the component States of the United States of America or the Cantons of the Swiss Republic. This is the main idea of many suggestions made for the maintenance of peace in the discussion of post-war reconstruction.

There can be no doubt that the ideal solution of the problem of world organization as the problem of world peace is the establishment of a World Federal State composed of all or as many nations as possible. The realization of this idea, however, is confronted with serious and, at least at present, insurmountable difficulties.

The first problem concerns the way in which a World State may be established. Those who propound this idea usually think of an international treaty by which States, previously sovereign subjects of international law, submit themselves to a federal constitution the terms of which form the contents of the treaty. This is the only democratic way to establish the World State.

The suggestion to secure international peace through a World State is based on the analogy assumed to exist between a World State and the national State by which national peace is so effectively secured. This analogy, however, seems to be not very favorable to the intentions of those who wish to bring about the peace of the world by methods which comply with the principles of democracy: liberty and equality, applied to international relations. For the national State with its effect of national peace is not the result of an agreement voluntarily negotiated by free and equal individuals. The supposition maintained by the natural law doctrine of the seventeenth and eighteenth centuries that the State originates in a social contract concluded by sovereign individuals in a state of nature long since has been abandoned and replaced by another hypothesis according to which the State comes into existence through hostile conflicts between social groups of different economic structure. In the course of these armed conflicts, which have the character of bloody wars, the most aggressive and warlike group subjugates the others and imposes upon them a peace order. The *pax romana* enjoined on the peoples vanquished by the Roman legions is the most striking example of a process which, according to this hypothesis, has taken place, though in smaller extent, in historic and prehistoric times in almost all parts of the world. The World State, so the followers of this doctrine of the origin of the State argue, can come into existence in no other way than any other State, that is, by forcible subjugation of all the nations of the world; and world peace can be established only in an order imposed upon mankind by one great Power. If world peace can be secured only by a World State, then the belief in the possibility of establishing such a State by an international treaty concluded by independent governments is, according to the force theory, just the same mistake as the natural law doctrine that the national State has been established by the voluntary agreement of individuals determined by their reasonable insight into the advantages of peaceful collaboration under an authority upon which the monopoly of force is conferred. History seems to teach that it is not the way of law, but the way of force, which leads to peace.

It is, however, more than probable that neither is the doctrine of the social contract entirely false nor is the theory of forcible subjugation entirely correct. If the former is a construction based on an optimistic evaluation of human nature rather than a historic explanation of the State's origin, the latter is evidently influenced by a pessimistic value judgment on the social evolution of the past. Since the first transition of primitive, highly decentralized groups to State organization is an event which occurred in prehistoric times, and the origin of many existing States is, due to the lack of historic sources, not a possible subject of scientific research, the hypotheses on this topic are always, at least partly, determined by considerations based on general psychology. From such a viewpoint, however, it seems very likely that no forcible subjugation of human beings can bring about a relatively lasting state of peace without a minimum of consent on the part of the subjugated people, be it only their feeling that the order established by their rulers is, after all, better than a state of permanent war. On the other hand, no social contract can constitute a more than temporarily pacified community without power to enforce the order constituting the community. Force and law do not exclude each other. Law is an organization of force.

The establishment by an international treaty of an international organization for the maintenance of peace is a transaction totally different from that to which the doctrine of the social contract refers. This doctrine is so problematical because it is hardly possible that in a state of nature prior to the existence of any law a contract could be made by thousands of contracting subjects, a contract legally binding not only upon them but also upon their wives and children and upon the yet unborn generations of the future. No contract concluded between individuals could have such an effect, especially if it is not made on the basis of a pre-existing legal order. The social contract of the natural law doctrine is in truth the act by which the law, the national law, first comes into existence; and it is not very likely that the law as such has been created by a contract.

The international treaty by which an international organization for the maintenance of peace would have to be established would be concluded on the basis of a legal order which has existed for many hundreds of years. The number of the contracting parties, compared with that of the fictitious contractors of the social compact, is very small. The contracting parties would be States, and would not necessarily change with every generation. The change of parties within the family of nations is not nearly so frequent as the change of persons within communities of men. It is a generally accepted principle of positive international law that States, and that means their subjects, are bound by international treaties without regard to the change of generations which takes place within the population of the States concerned.

The fact that the State did not originate in a social contract is not an argument against the possibility of establishing by an international treaty a peace securing order. Even if national peace secured by the national State were always and everywhere the result of forcible subjugation, there is no necessity of believing that this is the only way to establish international peace and that we must wait with our hope for a better world until one Leviathan has swallowed all the others. It may be that reasonable insight into the advantages of peaceful collaboration played no decisive role in the historical process through which, many thousands of years ago, the State first came into existence in a still primitive society. But this is no reason to underestimate the importance of that factor in the relationship between modern democratic States acting more and more under the influence of the public opinion of enlightened nations. It is a fact that agreement on an effective organization for the maintenance of peace is easier, the smaller the number of the parties whose consent is required. In this respect, the second World War seems to open better prospects than the first one. If, at the close of the second World War, only three or four Great Powers remain, and these are satisfied in their territorial claims, then the chance of a treaty establishing an effective international organization for the maintenance of peace, the idea of international peace through international law are indeed within the scope of practical politics.

2. World State or Confederacy of States?

THE ANALOGY between national and international peace implying the priority of the force theory over the contract doctrine in respect to inter-State relations is not conclusive for still another reason: international peace can be secured without the establishment of a World State. The high degree of centralization characteristic of the State is not, or will not be immediately after the close of this war, necessary to guarantee a durable peace. The force monopoly, the essential element of a legal community securing peace among its members, is possible even if the centralization of the community does not reach the degree characteristic of a State. By international treaties, it is true, even States can be and have been established, in particular federal States. A World Federal State, however, composed of many States different in size and culture, can hardly be erected immediately after this war. Only wishful thinking and ignorance of decisive facts allow us to underestimate the extraordinary

difficulties we must encounter in organizing such a World
Federal State; especially is this true if its constitution is to
have a democratic character. And it is for democracy that
the United Nations have accepted the sacrifices of this war.
The center of a democratic World State must be a world
parliament. But a world parliament in which all the United
Nations would be represented according to their aggregate
numerical strength would be a legislative body in which
India and China would have approximately three times as
many deputies as the United States of America and Great
Britain together. The central organs of the World State
would have about the same jurisdiction as the federal government in the United States. Hence the United States,
which is itself a federal State, could not become a member
of the World Federal State without a radical change in its
own constitution. The government of a sovereign State is
by its very nature inclined to resist any restriction upon its
independence; and to become a member of a federal State
means giving up completely one's independence. The resistance against such a State suicide must, of course, reach the
highest degree immediately after a victorious war, which inevitably increases the nationalistic feelings of people.

Certainly the limits on self-determination which a federal
constitution imposes upon member States have to be
weighed against the great advantages of centralization. But
these advantages weigh little when the right of self-determination is in question, the right of self-determination of a
people imbued with a strong feeling of nationalism, especially if this feeling is based on the possession of a common
language, religion, culture, and a long and glorious history.
Opinions may differ as to the value and justification of nationalism; but one must reckon with this phenomenon as
with other decisive facts if one is considering the establish-

ment of a universal community of States. This is especially true if the international community is to comprise nations so different from one another in respect to language, religion, culture, history, political and economic structure, and in their geographic situation as are States of the American and States of the European continent, nations of western and nations of eastern civilizations.

If a federal State comprising all these States is proposed, the examples of the United States of America and Switzerland are usually referred to in order to show that the difficulties are not insuperable. But these examples prove little. In both instances, there had long existed close historical-political relations among the members which were ultimately united into a federal State. In both cases a mere confederacy had immediately preceded the federal State. In the case of the United States, essentially an English-speaking, preponderantly Protestant population was involved; their common economic and political interests led to the common political act of breaking away from the British mother country. The Swiss federal State, it is true, does present a union of several ethnic groups very different as to language and culture. But it was only insignificantly small portions of the German, French, and Italian nations separated from these nations by historical and political circumstances, not these mighty nations themselves, that united to form a relatively centralized community. And this community is probably held together less by inner forces than by the external pressure that the political system of the great powers neighboring Switzerland bring to bear on this little State. A radical change in the mutual relations of these powers would be decisive for the existence of the Swiss federal State. Finally, it must not be overlooked that, in the case of Switzerland as in that of the United States, geographically contiguous territories were united to form the territory of a single State, and that on this score alone it is quite a different proposition to unite into a single State States of all the continents separated as they are by two oceans. To base the hope of the erection of such a federal World State upon nothing more than the examples of the United States and Switzerland is a dangerous illusion.

Still, the aim must not be regarded as unattainable. It is quite possible that the idea of a universal World Federal State will be realized, but only after a long and slow development equalizing the cultural differences between the nations of the world, especially if this development is furthered by conscious political and educational work in the ideological field. At present, however, such a World State is not within the scope of political reality, for it is also incompatible with the "principle of sovereign equality" upon which, according to the Declaration signed by the governments of the United States, United Kingdom, the Soviet Union and China on November 1, 1943, at Moscow, the international organization to be established after the war shall be based.* If one accepts a World State as a desirable aim, it is more than likely that it can be reached only by a series of stages. From a strategic point of view, there is but one serious question: What is the next step to be taken with a view to success on this road? Obviously, at first only an international union of States, not a federal State, could be set up.

That means that the solution of the problem of a durable peace can be sought only within the framework of international law—that is to say, by an organization which, in the degree of its centralization, does not exceed that of the usual type of international communities. These communities are characterized by the fact that the law regulating the mutual

* *New York Times*, November 2, 1943. Cf. *infra*, pp. 34 ff.

relations of the member States retains its international character without being converted into national law. The constitution of a World State with a world government and a world parliament, however, although international law as the contents of an international treaty, is at the same time national law, since it is the basis of the law of the World State.

3. International judiciary

A CAREFUL EXAMINATION of the nature of international relations and the specific technique of international law shows a basic difficulty confronting every attempt to pacify relations between States. It is the fact that in case of disputes between States there exists no authority accepted generally and obligatorily as competent to settle international conflicts, that is, to answer impartially the question as to which of the parties to the conflict is right and which is wrong. If the States do not reach an agreement or do not voluntarily submit their dispute to arbitration, each State is authorized to decide for itself the question of whether the other State has violated, or is about to violate its right; and the State which considers itself injured is authorized to enforce the law—and that means what it considers to be the law—by resorting to war or reprisals against the alleged wrongdoer. Since the other State has the same competence to decide for itself the question of law, the fundamental legal problem remains without authoritative solution. The objective examination and unbiased decision of the question of whether or not the law has been violated is the most important, the essential stage in any legal procedure. As long as it is not possible to remove from the interested States the prerogative to answer the question of law and transfer it once and for all to an impartial authority, namely, an international court, any further progress on the way to the pacification of the world is absolutely excluded.

Consequently, the next step on which our efforts must be contentrated is to bring about an international treaty concluded by as many States as possible, victors as well as vanquished, establishing an international court endowed with compulsory jurisdiction. This means that all the States of the League constituted by this treaty are obliged to renounce war and reprisals as means of settling conflicts, to submit all their disputes without exception to the decision of the court, and to carry out its decisions in good faith.*

* For many years the writer has tried to show that the establishment of a court with compulsory jurisdiction is the first and indispensable step to an effective reform of international relations. Cf. H. Kelsen, *The Legal Process and International Order*, The New Commonwealth Research Bureau Relations, Series A, No. 1, London (1934); *Law and Peace in International Relations*, Oliver Wendell Holmes Lectures, Harvard University Press (1941); "Essential Conditions of International Justice," *Proceedings of the 35th Annual Meeting of the American Society of International Law* (1941), pp. 70 ff.; "International Peace by Court or Government," *The American Journal of Sociology* (1941), Vol. 46, pp. 571 ff.; "Discussion of Post War Problems," *Proceedings of the American Academy of Arts and Sciences* (1942), Vol. 75, No. 1, pp. 11 ff.; "Revision of the Covenant of the League of Nations," *World Organization, A Symposium of the Institute on World Organization* (1942), pp. 392 ff.; "Compulsory Adjudication of International Disputes," *American Journal of International Law* (1943). Vol. 37, pp. 397 ff.; "Peace through Law," *Journal of Legal and Political Sociology* (1943), Vol. 2, pp. 52 ff.; "The Strategy of Peace," *The American Journal of Sociology* (1944), Vol. 49, pp. 381 ff.

Since the outbreak of World War II the claim for an international court with compulsory jurisdiction as a means for the maintenance of law and peace has been supported by American public opinion to a steadily increasing degree. The American Branch of the International Law Association, the American Foreign Law Association, and the Federal Bar Association have adopted the following Resolution:

    1. That a primary war and peace objective of the United Nations is the establishment and maintenance at the earliest possible moment of an effective international peace among all nations based on law and the orderly administration of justice.

    2. That the administration of international justice requires the

Such a treaty can be concluded immediately after the war has come to an end; it can be concluded also with the vanquished States, whereas more ambitious agreements concerning world organization, especially with the defeated States, can be negotiated only after a rather long-lasting transitional period during which the Axis powers, after complete disarmament, are kept under the political and military control of the United Nations.

We may expect that Soviet Russia, too, will join an international League whose only purpose is to maintain peace within the community by establishing a court with compulsory jurisdiction. But we have no reason to believe that a Soviet government will enter a League which imposes upon its members obligations other than the duties not to resort to war or reprisals against another member, to submit all their conflicts to the decision of a court, and to execute the judicial decisions. To have Soviet Russia within, and not outside the international organization to be established after this war is essential to future peace.

---

organization of a judicial system of interrelated permanent international courts with obligatory jurisdiction.

3. That instrumentalities, agencies and procedures should be instituted and developed to declare and make effective the considered will of the community of Nations.

Somewhat similar resolutions were adopted by the House of Delegates of the American Bar Association. The Federal Council of Churches of Christ in America (New York), the National Catholic Welfare Conference (Washington) and the Synagogue Council of America adopted a common Catholic, Jewish, and Protestant Declaration on World Peace, Point 5 of which runs as follows:

International institutions to maintain peace with justice must be organized. An enduring peace requires the organization of international institutions which will (a) develop a body of international law, (b) guarantee the faithful fulfillment of international obligations, and revise them when necessary, (c) assure collective security by drastic limitations and continuing control of armaments, compulsory arbitration and adjudication of controversies, and the use when necessary of adequate sanctions to enforce the law.

4. Economic or juridical approach?

To ELIMINATE WAR, the worst of all social evils, from inter-
State relations by establishing compulsory international
jurisdiction, the juridical approach to an organization of the
world must precede any other attempt at international reform. Among the two aspects of the post-war problem, the
economic and legal, the latter has a certain priority over the
former. It is not too far-going a simplification to say that all
the difficulties and absurdities in international economic
relations originate almost exclusively in the possibility of
war, that is, in the fact that one government is afraid of, the
other is hoping for, war, and in consequence both attempt
to transform their countries into economically self-sufficient
bodies. When the possibility of war is really eliminated
from international relations, when no government has to
fear any disadvantage, and no government has to hope for
any advantage whatever brought about by war, the greatest
obstacle in the way to a reasonable reform of the economic
situation will disappear, at least insofar as the improvement
of the economic situation is an international, and not a national problem. It is not true that war is the consequence of
unsatisfactory economic conditions; on the contrary, the
unsatisfactory situation of world economy is the consequence of war. "Fear of war," writes an outstanding
economist, Mr. Pigou, "is both directly and through its in-
direct influence on policy, one of its principal causes." * It is

* A. C. Pigou, *The Political Economy of War* (1941), p. 28. Pigou says
(p. 18): "In a world liable to war it may not only happen, but it may be
wise for a country to sacrifice something of opulence in normal times in
order to protect itself against a shortage of food or other essential goods
should war break out. If the shadow of war were removed, this sacrifice of
opulence to defence would not be required."

a specific Marxian theory that the occurrence of war is exclusively or, at least predominantly, due to economic causes, especially to the capitalistic system. In his excellent study on the economic causes of war, Robbins has shown that this theory "does not stand up to the test of facts." * It would be, of course, an exaggeration to say that wars have no economic causes. Conflicts of national economic interest may indeed lead to war, † but they are not the root cause. "The ultimate condition giving rise to those clashes of national economic interest which lead to international war"—thus Robbins formulates the conclusion of his essay—"is the existence of independent national sovereignties. Not capitalism"—and this applies to any other economic system or situation—"but the anarchic political organization of the world is the root disease of our civilization." ‡ If the his-

* Lionel Robbins. *The Economic Causes of War* (1940), pp. 15 ff., 57,
† J. H. Jones. *Economics of War and Conquest* (1915), p. 160. says: "Although a war of conquest is likely to bring some return of wealth, and *may*, over a long period, bring a return commensurate with the outlay. the *chance* of a gain equal to or greater than the cost is never adequate compensation for the outlay itself. Even if he proved the chance of gain to be of greater material value than the certain loss, the conqueror. as already stated, would not have justified his action. Economic considerations should be entirely subordinated to other considerations. And in almost all international questions which endanger peace in the West it is probable that economic questions do occupy a subordinate position." Cf. also Quincy Wright, *A Study of War* (1942), Vol. II, pp. 717 ff., 1284 ff.
‡ Robbins, *op. cit.*, p. 99. Robbins says, pp. 104 ff.: "In the sense in which cause may be said to be a condition in the absence of which subsequent events could not have happened, the existence of independent sovereign states ought be justly regarded as the fundamental cause of conflict. ... In the sense which is significant for political action. it is the chaos of independent sovereignties which is the ultimate condition of international conflict. It is not only because the independent states have the power to declare war, that war is sometimes declared, it is also because they have the power to adopt policies involving clashes of national interest of which war seems the only solution.—If it is so, then the remedy is plain. Independent sovereignty must be limited. ... We know today that unless we destroy the sovereign state, the sovereign state will destroy us." It is of the greatest im-

tory of the last thirty years has taught us anything, it is the primacy of politics over economics. The elimination of war is our paramount problem. It is a problem of international policy, and the most important means of international policy is international law. .

Now we have already an international legal instrument excluding war from international relations, the so-called Briand-Kellogg Pact, ratified by almost all the nations of the world. At this moment that general treaty for the renunciation of war seems to be a rather weighty argument against a legal approach to the problem of peace. The failure of the Briand-Kellogg Pact, however, is due to its own technical insufficiency. On the one hand, the Pact attempted too much by prohibiting any kind of war, even war as a reaction against a violation of law, without replacing this sanction of international law by another kind of sanction, an internationally organized sanction; thus it favored States inclined to violate the rights of other States. On the other hand, the Pact undertook too little by obliging the States to seek pacific settlement of their disputes without obliging them to submit all their conflicts without any exception to the compulsory jurisdiction of an international court.

------

portance that these statements are the result of a scientific research into the economic causes of war, that an economist recognizes a political fact, the unlimited sovereignty of the States, as the decisive cause of war. There can be little doubt that the remedy suggested by Robbins, limitation of sovereignty, is correct. The only question is, how to achieve this end. And this question must be understood as a problem of peace strategy if the suggested solutions shall not present a utopian scheme.

5. Judiciary without centralized executive power and legislation

THE FIRST OBJECTION to the suggestion of establishing a court with compulsory jurisdiction concerns the execution of the court's decisions in the event that a State does not fulfill its obligation to obey the court or does resort to war or reprisals in disregard of its covenants. It is evident that the most effective method of enforcing the orders and judgments of the court is the organization of a centralized executive power, that is, an international police force different and independent from the armed forces of the member States, and to place this armed force at the disposal of a central administrative agency whose function is to execute the decisions of the court. An international police force is effective only if based on the obligation of the member States to disarm or radically to limit their own armament, so that solely the League is permitted to maintain an armed force of considerable strength. A police force of this kind is "international" only with respect to its legal basis, the international treaty. It is, however, "national" with respect to the degree of its centralization, for a League with a centralized executive power is no longer an international confederacy of States but a State itself.

There can be no doubt that the attempt to organize such a police force must reckon with the stubborn resistance of the governments; and the international treaty establishing the international police force must obtain the ratification of all governments concerned. A public opinion more or less favorable to the organization of a world police is not sufficient. A so-called "international" police force is a radical restriction, if not the total destruction, of the sovereignty of the States. It is incompatible with the principle of "sovereign equality" proclaimed by the Declaration of Moscow.

The organization of a centralized executive power, the most difficult of all the problems of world organization, cannot be the first step—it can only be one of the last steps, a step which in any case cannot successfully be undertaken before the international court has been established, and has, by its impartial activities, gained the confidence of the governments. For then, and then only, sufficient guarantees will be given that the armed force of the League would be used exclusively to maintain the law according to the judgment of an impartial authority.

As long as the Covenant constituting the international court does not establish a central armed force, the decisions of the international court can be executed against a reluctant State only by the other States, members of the international community, if necessary by the use of their own armed forces under the direction of the previously mentioned administrative agency. This administrative agency may be authorized by the Covenant to appoint an official whose function should be to control the military obligations of the member States, and, if a military sanction is to be executed according to the decision of the court, to appoint a commander-in-chief of the League. The fact that the main task of the administrative body will be to execute the decisions of the court will facilitate considerably its organization, especially with respect to its procedure. For the resolutions by which the administrative council carries out the decisions of the court must be adopted by the majority of its members, and need not require unanimity as did the decisions of the Council of the League of Nations.

As a matter of fact, in the field of international relations the majority principle is not applied—with one exception.

The exception is extremely significant, however; it is the procedure of international courts. Here, and here alone, is the majority vote principle generally accepted. Submission to the majority vote of an international court is not considered incompatible with the sovereignty of a State. This is one of the reasons why it is advisable to make a court, and not a government, the main instrument of an international reform. It is the line of least resistance.

Another reason is the fact that treaties of arbitration have proved until now the most effective. Seldom has a State refused to execute the decision of a court to whose authority it has submitted itself in a treaty. The idea of law, in spite of everything, still seems to be stronger than any other ideology of power.

A third reason is furnished by the history of law. The problem of world organization is a problem of centralization; and the whole evolution of the law from its primitive beginnings to its standard of today has been, from a technical point of view, a continuous process of centralization. In the field of municipal law this process is characterized by the surprising fact that the centralization of the law-applying function—that is, the establishment of courts—precedes the centralization of the law-creating function—the establishment of legislative organs. Long before parliaments as legislative bodies came into existence, courts were established to apply the law to concrete cases. It is a characteristic fact that the meaning of the term "parliament" originally was court.

In primitive society the courts were hardly more than tribunals of arbitration. They had to decide only whether or not the delict had actually been committed as claimed by one party, and hence, if the conflict could not be settled by peaceful agreement, whether or not one party was authorized to execute a sanction against the other according to the principle of self-help. Only at a later stage did it become possible completely to abolish the procedure of self-help and to replace it by execution of the court-decision through a centralized executive power, a police force of the State. The centralization of the executive power is the last step in this evolution from the decentralized pre-State community to the centralized community we call State. We have good reason to believe that international law—that is, the law of the inter-State community, completely decentralized and dominated by the principle of self-help—develops in the same way as the primitive law of the pre-State community. If this is true, we can with a certain degree of probability foresee the direction in which a relatively successful attempt may be undertaken to secure international peace, to eliminate the principle of self-help from international law by emphasizing and strengthening the given tendency toward centralization. Natural evolution tends first toward international judiciary, and not toward international government or legislation.

This settles another objection which is continually brought against the establishment of a compulsory international jurisdiction, namely, that the international legal order to be applied by the court is deficient and that international jurisdiction is not possible without an international legislative body competent to adapt international law to the changing circumstances. From the fact that it is impossible to form such a legislative body it is concluded that a compulsory international jurisdiction is also impossible.

This argument is incorrect in every respect. As pointed out, the development of national law indicates on the contrary that the obligation to submit to the decision of the courts long precedes legislation, the conscious creation of law by a central organ. Within the individual State courts have for centuries applied a legal order which could not be changed by any legislator, but which developed, exactly like present-day international law, out of custom and agreements; and in this legal system custom was for the most part formed by the practice of the courts themselves. An international court which exercises the jurisdiction of deciding all the legal disputes of those parties subject to the law, even if it is empowered by the constitution to apply only the positive law, gradually and imperceptibly will adapt this law in its concrete decisions to actual needs. The history of Roman and Anglo-American law shows how judicial decisions create law. A famous American jurist has said: "All the law is judge made law." * This statement goes perhaps too far. But it saves us from overestimating the function of legislation, and makes us understand why there can be no legislator without a judge, even though there can very well be a judge without a legislator.

6. Legal and political conflicts

IN CLOSE CONNECTION with the argument of the inadequacy of the law to be applied by the international tribunal is the distinction between legal and political conflicts. This distinction is made to justify the exclusion of some international disputes from the jurisdiction of international tribunals. It is said that these disputes are by their very nature exempt from submission to binding judicial decisions, and that they are "political" and therefore not justiciable disputes, in contradistinction to others which are "legal" and

* John C. Gray, *The Nature and Sources of the Law* (2nd ed., 1927), p. 125.

therefore justiciable. Sometimes it is even said that the ma-
jor sources of international conflicts are economic or political and not legal in character, that law plays only a minor
part in international social control, and that consequently
the place of courts in international relations is *a priori* restricted. The latter argument implies a fallacy. Any conflict between States as well as between private persons is
economic or political in character; but that does not exclude treating the dispute as a legal dispute. A conflict is
economic or political with respect to the interests which are
involved; it is legal (or non-legal) with respect to the nor-
mative order controlling these interests. If A claims an estate which is in the possession of B and B refuses to comply
with A's claim, the dispute is economic in character; but to
say that this dispute is not legal *because* it is economic is
obviously absurd. It makes no difference that A and B are
States and that the dispute concerns, instead of an estate, a
part of the territory of B.

Territorial disputes are usually considered to be "political" *par excellence.* In a boundary controversy between
Rhode Island and Massachusetts which was brought before
the Supreme Court in 1838, objection was made to the jurisdiction of the court on the ground that the controversy was
political and not legal. This contention was, however,
denied by the United States Supreme Court. In his decision Mr. Justice Baldwin declared: "All controversies
between nations are, in this sense, political, and not judicial, as none but the sovereign can settle them," but
"there is neither the authority of law nor reason for the
position, that boundary between nations or states, is, in
its nature, any more a political question than any other
subject on which they may contend..." He then com-
mented upon political and legal questions as follows:

We are thus pointed to the true boundary line between political and judicial power, and questions. A sovereign decides by his own will, which is the supreme law within his own boundary; 6 Peters, 714; 9 Peters, 748; a court, or judge, decides according to the law prescribed by the sovereign power, and that law is the rule for judgment. The submission by the sovereigns, or states, to a court of law or equity, of a controversy between them, without prescribing any rule of decision, gives power to decide according to the appropriate law of the case; 11 Ves. 294; which depends on the subject matter, the source and nature of the claims of the parties, and the law which governs them. From the time of such submission, the question ceases to be a political one to be decided by the *sic volo, sic jubeo,* of political power; it comes to the court to be decided by its judgment, legal discretion, and solemn consideration of the rules of law appropriate to its nature as a judicial question, depending on the exercise of judicial power; as it is bound to act by known and settled principles of national or municipal jurisprudence, as the case requires.*

---

* 12 Peters 657, 737. The case is quoted by George A. Finch, Director of the Carnegie Endowment for International Peace, in the *Annual Report for 1943 of the Division of International Law,* p. 11. Mr. Finch says: "It need not be emphasized that in any planning for a post-war world based on law and order, an international court of justice must be part of the proposed structure. In the Director's opinion, the greatest defect of previous attempts at international organization has been the undue emphasis placed upon the settlement of international disputes by political bodies and the minimizing of the greater effectiveness with which many so-called political questions might be dealt with if reduced to legal terms and referred to an international court." Having called attention to the above quoted decision of the Supreme Court, Mr. Finch states: "It is interesting to observe in this connection that the meticulous attempts to draw fine distinctions in the modes of settlement between legal and political questions have grown out of the present-century efforts to formulate stipulations for the obligatory arbitration of future disputes. Such distinctions find no place in the numerous *ad hoc* arbitrations of prior disputes which took place during the preceding centuries. The United States has been a party to the arbitration of a number of important boundary disputes with other nations. Great Britain certainly did not consider that the Alabama

If relations between persons—private individuals or States —are regulated by a legal order at all, all possible conflicts between these persons, whether economic or political in character, are at the same time legal conflicts if judged by the legal order; and, objectively, they always can be judged by the legal order although, from the viewpoint of certain subjective interests, it may be undesirable to treat them as legal conflicts.

The statement that law plays a minor part in international social control, if taken literally, is meaningless. If positive international law is recognized as a system of legal rules regulating international relations, the part that this law plays in international affairs is neither less nor greater than the part which national law plays in national affairs. It may be that the part which international law plays in the relations between States is less satisfactory than the part which national law plays in the relations between private individuals. It cannot, however, be denied that national law, too, regulates many relations between private individuals unsatisfactorily. Nevertheless, no one would say that *therefore* national law plays only a minor part in national social control. There may be a qualitative difference between two legal systems insofar as one is more just than the other. A quantitative difference, however, in the sense that one system regulates more, the other fewer relations so that by the latter, more relations are not regulated than under the former, is excluded. The function of a legal system is to oblige the persons subjected to it to behave in a certain way

Claims controversy with the United States were anything but a political one, and it was necessary for the United States to stipulate in the treaty of arbitration the principles of law to be applied by the tribunal. Hundreds of other less known cases have been arbitrated by many countries involving a great variety of questions which might easily been classed as political and not legal if the will to arbitrate had not been present."

toward each other. If a person—private individual or State —is legally not obliged to behave in a certain way toward another person, the former is legally authorized to behave in this respect as he pleases to behave. What is legally not forbidden is legally permitted. If international law, customary or conventional, does not oblige State A to permit immigration to citizens of State B, State A is legally free to permit or not to permit immigration to citizens of State B, and it does not violate a right of State B by not permitting immigration to the latter's citizens. In this respect the relation between State A and State B is legally not less regulated than if international law, customary or conventional, obliged State A to permit immigration to citizens of State B. The relations which are within the sphere of that which is legally permitted are not less legally regulated than the relations that are within the sphere of that which is legally forbidden. On this point there is no difference between national and international law, and hence there is no reason to say that law plays a smaller part in international than in national social control. The true meaning of this statement is not, as it seems, the assertion of a fact, but rather the expression of a wish, namely, to eliminate, not international law, which is impossible, but international judiciary from certain relations between States, actually regulated by positive international law.

This is the real function of the distinction between legal and political conflicts thus as it is defined by the well-known formula of the Locarno Treaties of 1925: Legal disputes are disputes in which the parties are in conflict as to their respective legal rights, whereas all other disputes are political disputes. This definition is not satisfactory. It refers only to legal rights, although disputes concern in the first place legal duties. The Locarno formula creates the false impression that the difference between legal and political disputes refers to the matter of the conflict and, consequently, that legal disputes can be distinguished from political ones by an objectively ascertainable quality inherent in the conflict. This is not true. The difference consists in the way the parties to the conflict justify their respective attitudes. The criterion is, therefore, purely subjective. Legal disputes are disputes in which both parties base their respective claims and their rejection of the other party's claim on positive international law; whereas political disputes are disputes in which at least one party bases its claim or its defense, not on positive international law, but on other principles or on no principle at all.

If an international treaty, establishing the jurisdiction of an international tribunal for the settlement of international conflicts, recognizes a difference between legal and political conflicts, and if this treaty subjects only the legal conflicts to the jurisdiction of the tribunal, the effect of such a provision is that every State has it in its power to withdraw any conflict whatever from the jurisdiction of the tribunal and thus rid itself of its obligation to submit at least some of its conflicts with other States to the jurisdiction of the tribunal. For the legal or political character of a conflict depends exclusively on the discretion of the parties. If State A claims a part of the territory of State B, and B refuses to comply with A's claim, and if both base their respective attitude on existing positive international law, then, and then only, the conflict is a legal conflict. If, however, A bases its claim not on positive international law (and that implies that A recognizes that according to positive international law B has a legal right to the territory in question or, at least, that A does not deny B's legal right), then the conflict is a political conflict. The same is true when B bases its rejection of A's claim (based on positive law) not on positive law, which implies that B recognizes or, at least, does not deny that A has a legal right to claim the territory in question. If one party to a conflict wishes to avoid the jurisdiction of a tribunal competent to settle legal conflicts, it needs only to recognize or not to deny the legal right of the other party and justify its claim or its rejection of the other party's claim by principles of justice and the like, or maintain its attitude without any justification at all. The tribunal, too, must recognize the political character of .a dispute if one party justifies its conflicting attitude to the other party in another way than by invoking positive international law.

To claim something or to reject another's claim without basing one's attitude on positive law and thus recognizing or not denying the other party's legal right normally implies that the party which bases its attitude not on positive law considers the latter unsatisfactory, unjust, and the like, and therefore wishes that the law should be changed. This does not imply, as is sometimes assumed, that there is no rule of positive law according to which the conflicts can be settled, that, consequently, positive law cannot be applied to the conflict. Such a situation is impossible. A positive legal order can always be applied to any conflict whatever. Only two cases are possible: either the legal order contains a rule obliging one party to behave as the other party demands, or the legal order contains no such rule. In the first case, the application of the legal order to the conflict has the effect of admitting the claim; in the second case, the application of the legal order has the effect of rejecting the claim. The rule system of the international legal order is applicable in both cases; and consequently, political as well as legal conflicts are justiciable in the true sense of the term, indicating that they can be settled by a judicial decision applying positive law to the conflict. But the effect resulting from the application of the existing legal rules may be, from some points of view, unsatisfactory, in the first as well as in the second case. Hence, to declare that a conflict is political implies only that the party which bases its claim or the dismissal of the other party's claim not on positive law, considers the latter unsatisfactory, unjust, and the like.

If an international treaty establishing the jurisdiction of a tribunal for the settlement of conflicts recognizes the distinction between legal and political conflicts, it authorizes the parties to the conflict to withdraw any conflict from the jurisdiction of the tribunal whenever the party considers the application of the law to the conflict to be unsatisfactory. Consequently, the effect of a clause admitting only legal conflicts to the jurisdiction of an international tribunal is to annul the stipulation obliging the State to submit conflicts to the jurisdiction of the tribunal. This effect is all the more paradoxical since the restriction of the tribunal's jurisdiction to legal conflicts authorizes the party to escape the jurisdiction precisely in the event that this party recognizes or, at least, does not deny the other party's legal right. The distinction between legal and political conflicts plays a role analogous to that of the ill-famed *clausula rebus sic stantibus* (the doctrine that an international treaty ceases to be binding as soon as the circumstances under which it has been concluded are essentially altered). Just as the latter invalidates the rule *pacta sunt servanda* (treaties are binding), so does the former abolish the duty of obligatory jurisdiction.

The opinion of a party that the law which the tribunal has to apply to the conflict is unsatisfactory cannot be a legitimate reason for excluding the conflict from judicial decision or arbitration, that is, from the application of the existing law. For such an opinion is based on a subjective value judgment of the interested party. And even if there were a more or less objective criterion for determining the alleged insufficiency of the law—which there is not—such insufficiency could never justify the non-application of the law. For this law is, according to a generally accepted doctrine, recognized by all the States of the international community and thus also by the parties to the conflict. It is on this recognition that the doctrine bases the binding force of international law. Its non-application leads to anarchy and not to the change in the law which apparently is wanted by a party that declares a conflict to be political.

The exclusion of so-called political disputes from the jurisdiction of international tribunals cannot be compensated for by submitting these disputes to conciliation through non-judicial agencies, such as the Council of the League of Nations. Since it is possible that no unanimity and even no majority may be obtained for a positive recommendation for settlement of the conflict and, since, if obtained, the recommendation made by the organ of conciliation is not binding upon the parties, conciliation does not necessarily lead to a settlement of the conflict. This is true also if a unanimous decision of the organ of conciliation has binding force upon the parties.* The cases in which

* In *The International Law of the Future. Postulates, Principles, Proposals. A Statement of a Community of Views by North Americans* (International Conciliation, April, 1944, No. 399), the distinction between legal and political disputes is maintained. Proposal 17 runs as follows: " (1) The Permanent Court of International Justice should have jurisdiction over all disputes in which States are in conflict as to their respective legal rights and which are not pending before the Executive Council, such jurisdiction to be exercised upon an application by any party to the dispute ..." Proposal 18: " (1) Acting upon its own initiative or at the request of any State, the Executive Council should have power to take cognizance of any dispute between two or more States which is not pending before the Permanent Court of International Justice. (2) The Executive Council should have power to take such measures as it may deem to be necessary for preventing an aggravation or extension of the dispute; and, by major-

unanimity can be reached within a more or less political
body are very rare. Nothing is more dangerous to peace
than the existence of a conflict which is not settled and for
the peaceful settlement of which no obligatory procedure
is provided. Such a situation is the greatest temptation for
settling the conflict by the employment of force, even if
force as a means of settling conflicts is forbidden by a special
treaty. The complete failure of the Briand-Kellogg Pact
clearly shows that it is useless to outlaw war without elimi-
nating the possibility of legally unsettled and unsettleable
conflicts. To maintain this dangerous possibility is the true
function of the distinction between legal and political conflicts.

7. Conciliation

COMPULSORY JURISDICTION of an international court does
not exclude a procedure of conciliation. If the parties agree,
the conflict may first be submitted to a commission of conciliation. Then the court becomes competent only in the
event of failure of conciliation. This is provided by Article

---

ity vote, to request an advisory opinion of the Permanent Court of International Justice on any legal question connected with the dispute. (3) If
its effort to bring about a settlement of the dispute by the agreement of
the parties is not successful, the Executive Council should have power,
by unanimous vote, to give a decision which will be binding on the parties; failing such a decision, it should have power, by majority vote, to
adopt and publish a report containing a statement of the facts and the
recommendations deemed to be just and proper in regard thereto...."

If the Executive Council cannot reach a unanimous vote the dispute
remains unsettled. This is the principle which underlies also Articles 12-15
of the Covenant of the League of Nations. The proposals of *The International Law of the Future* aim at a remarkable progress in relationship to
the respective provisions of the Covenant of the League of Nations only
in so far as a unanimous decision of the Executive Council should be
binding on the parties which, consequently, would be obliged to execute
the decision; whereas a unanimous report of the Council of the League
of Nations has merely the effect that war against the party which complies
with the recommendations is expressly forbidden.

20 of the General Act of 1928 for the Pacific Settlement of International Disputes. The General Act submits also political disputes to judicial decision (Articles 21-28). But this progress is completely neutralized by the stipulation of Article 39, which allows the States to make their acceptance of the General Act conditional upon reservations. Among the reservations admitted by the General Act, the most problematical is that referring to "questions which by international law are solely within the domestic jurisdiction of States." This is the well known formula of Article 15, Section 8, of the Covenant of the League of Nations, a formula which is very much contested. There are no questions which, by their very nature, are "solely within the domestic jurisdiction" of a State. Any matter may become the object of an international treaty and thus cease to be solely within the domestic jurisdiction of the contracting States. A matter is "solely" within the domestic jurisdiction of a State only so long as it is not subject to a norm of customary or conventional international law. But this does not mean that such a matter cannot be the cause of an international conflict or that international law cannot be applied to such a conflict. For a dispute between States to arise out of a matter which "by international law is solely within the domestic jurisdiction" of one of the parties means nothing else but that international law does not obligate the party to behave in the way claimed by the other party and consequently that the former has, according to international law, a right to repudiate the claim of the latter. The statement that a matter out of which an international dispute has arisen is solely within the domestic jurisdiction of one of the parties implies the application of international law to this case; for it is "by international law," according to Article 15, Section 8, of the Covenant of the League of Nations, as

well as Article 39 of the General Act, that the matter is solely within the domestic jurisdiction of the party to a dispute. Hence, there is nothing in the nature of the case that could justify the exemption of such a dispute from the jurisdiction of an international court.

8. Sovereign equality of the States as basis of an international organization for the maintenance of peace

SINCE THE MOSCOW CONFERENCE has declared the principle of "sovereign equality" as the basis of the international organization to be established after this war, it is necessary to examine the question whether an international court with compulsory jurisdiction in the sense developed above is compatible with this principle.

The term "sovereign equality" probably means sovereignty and equality, two generally recognized characteristics of States as subjects of international law. To speak of sovereign equality is justified insofar as both qualities are usually considered to be connected with each other. The equality of States is frequently explained as a consequence of or as implied by their sovereignty.

What is the meaning of the very ambiguous term "sovereignty" as used in the Four Power Declaration? We may assume that in this declaration the term "sovereignty," usually defined as supreme authority, has a meaning not incompatible with the existence of international law imposing duties and conferring rights upon the States. For "the reestablishment of law and order and the inauguration of a system of general security" are, according to the same declaration, war aims of the Four Powers. The "law and order" to be re-established with the effect of inaugurating a system of general security can only be the law of nations, the international legal order as a set of norms binding upon the States. If it is assumed that the States have duties imposed and, consequently, rights conferred upon them by international law, they must be considered as subjected to international law. By the figurative expression "to be subjected" nothing else is meant than the relationship of subjects to a legal order imposing duties and conferring rights upon them. The sovereignty of the States, as subjects of international law, is the legal authority of the States under the authority of international law. If sovereignty means "supreme" authority, the sovereignty of the States as subjects of international law cannot mean an absolutely, but only a relatively supreme authority; the State's legal authority is "supreme" insofar as it is not subjected to the legal authority of any other State. The State is "sovereign" since it is subjected only to international law, not to the national law of any other State. The State's sovereignty under international law is the State's legal independence from other States. This is the usual significance attributed to the term "sovereignty" by writers on international law.

Sovereignty is sometimes defined as supreme "power." In this connection, power means the same as authority, namely, legal power, the competence to impose duties and confer rights. If "power" has not this meaning referring to the realm of norms or values, but rather the meaning "capability of producing an effect," a meaning referring to the realm of reality determined by laws of causality, then it is easy to show that sovereignty as a supreme power in this latter sense cannot be characteristic of States as legal entities. With respect to their actual power the various States differ very much from each other. Compared with and in

relationship to a so-called Great Power, a State like Lichten-
stein has no power at all, although it is also called a Power
in diplomatic phraseology. If "power" means actual power,
i.e., the capacity to bring about an effect, "supreme power"
would mean to be a first cause, a *prima causa*. In this sense,
only God as the Creator of the world is sovereign; this concept of sovereignty is a metaphysical, not a scientific one. But
the tendency to deify the State leads to a political theory
which is rather a theology than a science of the State, and in
this political theology the concept of sovereignty assumes a
metaphysical significance. Sovereignty in the sense of international law means the legal authority or competence of a
State limited and limitable only by international law, and
not by the national law of another State.

The term "equality" designating an essential characteristic of States as subjects of international law seems, at first
glance, to signify that all States have the same duties and the
same rights. This statement, however, is obviously not true,
since the duties and rights established by international
treaties constitute a great diversity among States. Consequently, the statement must be restricted to general customary international law. But even according to general
customary international law, all States have not the same
duties and rights. A littoral State has other duties and rights
than an inland State. The statement concerned is correct
only if modified as follows: according to general international law all States have the same capacity of being charged
with duties and of acquiring rights; equality does not mean
equality of duties and rights, but rather equality of capacity
for duties and rights. Equality is not unconditional equality
of duties and rights; it is the principle that, under the same
conditions, the States have the same duties and the same

rights. This, however, is an empty and insignificant formula since it is applicable even in case of radical inequalities. A rule of general international law conferring privileges on Great Powers could be interpreted as being in conformity with the principle of equality, since the rule can be represented as follows: any State, on the condition that it is a Great Power, enjoys the privileges concerned. The principle of equality, as formulated above, is but a tautological expression of the principle of legality, i.e., the principle that the general rules of law ought to be applied in all cases in which, according to their contents, they ought to be applied. This is the reason why the principle of legal equality, if nothing but the empty principle of legality, is compatible with any actual inequality.

It is therefore quite understandable that most of the writers on international law try to attribute a more substantial import to the concept of equality. When characterizing the States as equal, they mean that according to general international law no State can be legally bound without or against its will; that, consequently, international treaties are binding merely upon the contracting States; that the decision of an international agency is not binding upon a State which is not represented in the agency or whose representative has voted against the decision; that the majority vote principle is excluded from the realm of international law. Other applications of this principle of equality are the rules that no State has jurisdiction over another State (and that means over the acts of another State) without the latter's consent—*par in parem non habet imperium*—and that the courts of one State are not competent to question the validity of the acts of another State insofar as those acts purport to take effect within the sphere of validity of the latter State's national legal order. The principle of equality understood

in this way is the principle of autonomy of the States as subjects of international law.

According to the traditional doctrine, the equality of the
States in the sense of autonomy is derivable from their sovereignty. However, it is not possible to derive from the sovereignty of the State—that is, from the principle that a State
is subjected only to international law, not to the national
law of another State—the rules that no State can be legally
bound without or against its will, that international treaties
are binding only upon the contracting States, that a State
cannot be legally bound by the decision of an international
agency if it is not represented in this law-making body or if
the State's representative has voted against the decision,
that no State has jurisdiction over the acts of another State,
and so on. These rules may or may not be rules of positive
international law, and the sovereignty of the States could be
a consequence of these rules, not the rules a consequence
of the sovereignty.

It is an illusion to believe that legal rules can be derived
from a concept such as sovereignty or any other legal concept. Legal rules are valid only if they are created by legislation, custom, or treaty; and the legal rules constituting the
so-called equality of States are valid not because the States
are sovereign, but because these rules are norms of positive
international law. And they are, indeed, norms of positive
international law; but these norms have, according to the
same international law, important exceptions. There are
international treaties which, according to general international law, impose duties upon third States, for instance,
treaties establishing so-called international servitudes, or
treaties establishing a new State and imposing at the same
time obligations upon this State (Danzig, the Vatican State).
There are cases where a State has jurisdiction over the acts

of another State without the latter's consent. By a treaty an
international agency may be established in which only a
part of the contracting States are represented and this
agency may be authorized by the treaty to adopt by majority
vote norms binding upon all the contracting States. Such a
treaty is not incompatible with the concept of international
law or with the concept of the State as subject of international law; and such a treaty is a true exception to the rule
that no State can be legally bound without or against its
own will. It cannot correctly be said, as it usually is, that all
decisions of an agency established by an international treaty
are adopted with the consent of all the contracting parties
to the treaty and that, consequently, no decision is adopted
without or against the will of any of the States bound by the
decision. This is a fiction which is in open contradiction to
the fact that a State not represented in the agency may in no
way have expressed its will with reference to the decision,
and that one represented may have voted against the decision and thus expressly declared its opposite will.

The fact that a State by concluding the treaty has given
its consent to the competence of the agency established by
the treaty is quite compatible with the fact that the State
can change its will. However, this change of will is legally
irrelevant; the contracting State remains legally bound by
the treaty, even if it ceases to will what it declared to will at
the moment it concluded the treaty. Only at that moment
concordance of will of the contracting States is necessary in
order to create the duties and rights established by the
treaty. The fact that the contracting State remains legally
bound by the treaty without regard to a unilateral change
of will clearly proves that a State can be bound even against
its will, and that the autonomy of the State under international law is not, and cannot be, unlimited. The will whose

expression is an essential element of the conclusion of the treaty is not necessarily the same will which the State has, or has not, with respect to the decision adopted by the agency established by the treaty.

Since it is undoubtedly possible that such a treaty can be concluded by sovereign States on the basis of general international law, it is a misuse of the concept of sovereignty to maintain that it is incompatible with the sovereignty of the States as subjects of international law to establish an agency endowed with the competence to bind, by a majority vote, States represented or not represented in the law-making body. This is not a logical impossibility, as is supposed by those who base their arguments on the concept of sovereignty. But what is logically possible may be politically undesirable. By a treaty establishing an agency competent to make decisions binding upon the contracting States that are not represented in the law-making body or that have voted against the decision, the freedom of action of the contracting States is certainly much more restricted than by any other treaty. But the difference is only a quantitative, not a qualitative one, since under a legal order unlimited freedom of action is impossible. By the establishment of an agency endowed with true legislative power, an international community is constituted which differs from any other international community in the degree of its centralization. But this too, is only a relative, not an absolute, difference, since even this centralized community is based on an international treaty and consequently has an international character. It is not quite correct to say that such a community, because of its centralization, is a State and therefore, ceases to be an international community. There is no absolute borderline between these two kinds of communities, one of which is constituted by national, the other by international law, since there is no absolute borderline between the sphere of national and that of international law. National law can arise from international law as, for instance, the constitution of a federal State established by an international treaty. Such a constitution is national law since it is the basis of the law of a State; and it is at the same time international law since it is the contents of an international treaty. Only the dogmatic prejudice of a dualistic interpretation of the relationship between national and international law can prevent recognition of this fact. Neither the fact that a treaty establishing a legislative agency restricts the freedom of action of the contracting States, nor the fact that the community constituted by such a treaty is more centralized than other international communities are justifies the argument that the establishment of a legislative agency is incompatible with the nature of international law, or, what amounts to the same, with the sovereignty of the States. But it may be incompatible with the interest of the States whose governments do not wish to be restricted in their freedom of action by a relatively centralized international organization and therefore refuse to conclude a treaty constituting a centralized community.

We can, of course, define sovereignty as we please, and thus define it in a way that submission to any agency endowed with legislative power is incompatible with sovereignty. We can, however, derive from the concept of sovereignty nothing else than what we have purposely put into its definition. Consequently, the incompatibility derived from our definition means, at bottom, that something is incompatible with our wishes. It is a characteristic trick of a questionable, but among jurists a favored, method to present as logically impossible that which, in truth, is only politically undesired since it is at variance with certain in-

terests. This has been one of the most important functions
of the concept of sovereignty since the time when the
French writer Jean Bodin introduced the idea into the
theory of the State in order to prove that the power of his
king "cannot" be restricted because it is by its very nature
sovereign, and that means "the absolute and perpetual
power within a State." From his definition of sovereignty
he deduced the "rights of sovereignty" and thus secured
to the doctrine of sovereignty its tremendous successs.

The declaration that the Powers of the Moscow Conference intend to establish an international organization on
the principle of "the sovereign equality of all peace-loving
States" probably means that these Powers are not willing to
conclude a treaty constituting an international community
more centralized than such communities usually are. It certainly means that the governments concerned have not in
view the establishment of an international agency endowed
with legislative or executive power, an agency having the
character of a true government. As far as the governmental
functions of the future international community are concerned, whose task shall be to maintain the "system of
general security," we can hardly expect a more satisfactory
competence than that which the Covenant of the League of
Nations conferred upon the Council and the Assembly. Both
were hampered by the principle of sovereign equality care-
fully maintained by the Covenant, the principle that no
State can be bound without or against its will. Consequently
both agencies were able to adopt decisions binding upon the
members only by unanimous vote and, as a rule, with the
consent of the members whose interests were affected by the
decision.

It is a fact, as previously mentioned in this study, that the
sole international organs whose procedure is actually not

subjected to the rule that no State can be legally bound without or against its will, are international tribunals. These agencies are competent to adopt decisions by a majority vote, and their decisions are binding upon the States which have established the tribunal by an international treaty. But the contracting States are not "represented" in the tribunal. A person is legally "represented" by another person if the latter is bound by the instructions of the former. An international judge, in the true sense of the term, however, is, at least in principle, independent—in particular independent of the State by which he has been appointed. To be appointed by an authority does not necessarily imply to be subjected to that authority. An international "judge," in the true sense of the term, does not "represent" the State by which he has been appointed, in contradistinction to a member of an international government who represents "his" State—that is, that State which has appointed or delegated him—since he has to carry out the instructions given him by his State. A person has the character of a "judge" only if he is not legally bound by instructions of the government which has appointed him. There are international tribunals whose members are not or, at least, partly not, appointed by the States who may be bound by the decisions of the tribunal. For instance, the Permanent Court of International Justice, whose members are elected by the Council and the Assembly of the League of Nations, not by the contesting States; or a tribunal of arbitration composed equally of judges appointed by the contesting States and authorized to choose together a chairman or umpire.

The establishment of an international tribunal composed of judges who are not representatives of the contesting States and operating according to majority vote decisions binding upon the contesting States is generally considered to be compatible with the sovereignty and equality of the States. This is due to the idea that international tribunals are competent only to apply positive international law to the disputes they have to settle, that they cannot impose by their decisions new obligations or confer new rights upon the contesting States. It seems that the principle of sovereign equality is maintained, in the first place, to ward off the possibility of the imposition of new obligations upon an unwilling State.

Consequently, the establishment of a court with compulsory jurisdiction is not incompatible with this principle insofar as the court applies positive international law to the disputes submitted to its decisions. This holds true also with respect to the decisions of political conflicts since it is possible, as it has been shown above, to apply positive international law to so-called political conflicts. If States are not allowed to settle disputes (including so-called political disputes) by the employment of force, and if each State is obliged to submit any dispute whatever to judicial decision when the other party appeals to the court, then States are obliged to treat all their disputes as legal disputes. By the Briand-Kellogg Pact, the States have been obliged not to employ force for the settlement of disputes, political disputes included. The establishment of compulsory jurisdiction, which goes a step further, does not abolish the sovereign equality of the States in the sense in which the term is generally understood. It merely puts an end to the possibility of disputes which cannot be settled at all and thus remain, in spite of the Briand-Kellogg Pact, a permanent danger to the peace, only because the law to be applied to this conflict is considered by one or the other party to the conflict as unsatisfactory to its interests. The establishment of compulsory adjudication of international disputes is a means, perhaps the most effective means, of maintaining positive international law.

A court endowed with compulsory jurisdiction will not apply only and exclusively positive international law to the disputes submitted to its decisions, even if the court is not expressly authorized by its statute to apply other norms. As previously pointed out, it is probable that a court which has the power to decide all disputes without any exception will, in cases in which the strict application of positive law seems to be unsatisfactory to the judges, adapt the positive law to their idea of justice and equity. Then a new obligation may be imposed and a new right conferred upon the contesting States, so that the establishment of a court with compulsory jurisdiction may be considered as not compatible with the sovereign equality of the States, at least insofar as such a court does not apply only and exclusively positive international law; and it is difficult to prevent an international court endowed with compulsory jurisdiction from applying other norms than those of positive international law.

This is not a decisive argument against the compatibility of a court with compulsory jurisdiction with the principle of sovereign equality. Regarding the creation of new obligations by the decision of the court, there exists no fundamental difference between such a court and other international tribunals restricted to the application of positive law. The view that the decisions of such tribunals, although adopted according to the principle of majority vote by judges who are not exactly representatives of the States bound by the decision, are compatible with the sovereignty and equality of the States, is based on the idea that the application of positive law by a judicial decision has only a declaratory, not a constitutive, character, and that the application of law differs essentially from the creation of law. According to the traditional doctrine the law to be applied by the judicial decision exists prior to the decision; this pre-existing law is only disputed in the relationship between the parties to the conflict. The dispute may refer to facts (*quaestio facti*) or to the law (*quaestio juris*), i.e., to the existence of a general rule of law or to its interpretation. However, at the bottom, even a dispute contesting mere facts revolves about legal questions. It is not the existence or interpretation of a general rule of law which is disputed; it is the applicability of this rule in the concrete case which one party claims and the other party denies. That means that the individual norm, the concrete duty or right, is disputed and can or cannot be derived from the general rule according to whether the facts exist or do not. The traditional doctrine maintains that a judicial decision applying positive law does not create law; it only ends the dispute by establishing, in an authoritative way, the law valid for the case at hand. It transforms, so to speak, disputed law into undisputed and, finally, indisputable law by ascertaining the general or individual norm which, though objectively existing, is subjectively disputed by the parties. The fallacy of this doctrine is that the authoritative establishment of a disputed fact as well as a disputed rule of law is not merely a declaratory but a highly constitutive act. In case a fact is disputed, the judicial decision ascertaining that the fact has occurred in truth legally "creates" the fact and consequently constitutes the applicability of the general rule of law referring to the fact. In the sphere of law the fact "exists," even if in the sphere of nature the fact has not occurred. If a court of last instance declares that an individual has concluded with another individual a contract and has not fulfilled it, or that an individual has committed murder, the disputed nonfulfillment of contract or commission of murder are legal facts, even if in reality the defendant has not concluded a contract or the accused has not committed the murder. As a "legal" fact, that is, as a fact to which the law attaches certain consequences (duties, rights, sanctions), the fact and accordingly its consequences, are "created" by the judicial decision; and it is only as a legal fact that it counts. In case a general rule of law is disputed, because the existence or the meaning of the rule is doubtful, the decision of the court interpreting the legal order or a special rule of that order is not less creative than the authentic and definitive ascertainment of a fact as the essential condition of the application of a general legal rule. There is no absolute antagonism between application and creation of law, since even a law-applying act is at the same time a law-creating act.

There is, to be sure, a certain difference between a judicial decision applying an undisputed pre-existing rule of positive law to a dispute and a judicial decision applying a new, i.e., not pre-existing, rule, thus altering the existing law and adapting it to the changing circumstances. But this difference is not so strongly marked as it seems to be, since the interpretation of the positive law, necessarily connected with any act of applying the law, always implies more or less an alteration of the law. Ordinary national courts authorized to interpret the law and not to alter it nevertheless always work in the direction of a gradual evolution of the law. Consequently, the difference between an international court endowed with compulsory jurisdiction and, therefore, more inclined than other international tribunals to adapt the existing law to the changing circumstances, and other international courts is not so great that submission to the former could be refused because of not being compatible with the principle of the sovereign equality of

States. With regard to this principle, it is not the difference between courts with and courts without compulsory jurisdiction which is decisive; it is the essential difference which exists between the slow and almost imperceptible evolution of law through judicial decisions and the more or less drastic change of the law through legislative agencies, i.e., organs created for the sole purpose of substituting new law for old law. This difference explains why submission to legislative organs, but not submission to courts, is considered to be incompatible with the principle of sovereign equality. This principle works as a protection against quick and relatively important changes of the law, but not against all change, for the law, by its very nature, is a dynamic, not a static, system.

The true reason for the generally accepted view that submission to the decision of an international tribunal is not incompatible with the principle of sovereign equality is not so much the consideration that those tribunals cannot impose new obligations upon the contesting States; this effect is almost unavoidable. The reason for such a view is that judicial decisions are objective and impartial, and that they are not political decrees issued according to the principle, which is a negation of law, that might goes before right. Even if the decision of an international tribunal does not constitute the strict application of a pre-existing legal rule, it is supposed to be founded at least on the idea of law—that is, on a rule which, although not yet positive law, ought, according to the conviction of the independent judges, to become law and which really becomes positive law for the case settled by the particular judicial decision. It is the submission to the law, to the law not as a system of unchangeable values, but as a body of slowly and steadily changing norms, which is not incompatible with the principle of sovereign equality since it is only this law that guarantees the co-existence of the States as sovereign and equal communities.*

9. The experiences of the League of Nations

FINALLY, the proposition that the next and most important step toward international peace is the establishment of an international court with compulsory jurisdiction is confirmed by the experiences of the League of Nations. This union of States, which is so far the biggest international community founded to secure international peace, has failed completely. Its breakdown is attributable to various causes. One of the most important, if not the decisive, cause is a fatal fault of its construction, the fact that the authors of the Covenant placed at the center of this international organization not the Permanent Court of International Justice, but a kind of international government, the Council of the League of Nations. The Assembly of the League, its other organ, placed beside the Council, gives the impression

* A court with compulsory jurisdiction was the object of the Convention for the Establishment of a Central American Court of Justice, signed on December 20, 1907, at Washington by the Governments of the Republics of Costa Rica, Guatemala, Honduras, Nicaragua, and Salvador. Article I of the Convention reads as follows: "...and maintain a permanent tribunal which shall be called the 'Central American Court of Justice,' to which they bind themselves to submit all controversies or questions which may arise among them, of whatsoever nature and no matter what their origin may be, in case the respective Departments of Foreign Affairs should not have been able to reach an understanding." According to the Preamble, the Convention was concluded by the contracting States "for the purpose of efficaciously guaranteeing their rights and maintaining peace and harmony inalterably in their relations, without being obliged to resort in any case to the employment of force." Submission to the compulsory jurisdiction of the Court was not only considered as compatible with the sovereignty and equality of the contracting States but also as a means of guaranteeing their rights as sovereign and equal subjects of international law. The Convention was concluded only for ten years (Art. XXVII). The Court came to an end in 1918.

of an international legislature. The dualism of government and parliament was probably more or less distinctly present in the minds of the founders when they created the two main organs of the League.

It might have been foreseen from the very beginning that a world government would not succeed if its decisions had to be taken unanimously, binding no member against its will, and if there were no centralized power to execute them. It is not to be wondered at that a world parliament, or whatever the Assembly of the League of Nations may be called, can be of only nominal value if the principle of majority is almost completely excluded from its procedure. But the majority principle, excluded, as a rule, from the procedure of the Council and the Assembly, has been introduced without any difficulty into the constitution of the Permanent Court of International Justice.

A critical analysis of the Covenant and an impartial examination of the activity of the League shows that it would have been more correct to make the principal organ an international court rather than an international administrative organ. Of all the political tasks entrusted to the League by its constitution, only the function stated in Articles 12 to 17, concerning the settlement of disputes, has been fulfilled with any degree of success. The results obtained in this field were not, however, in proportion to the extensiveness of the organization or its bureaucratic machinery. The reason is that neither an international administrative organ, such as the Council of the League of Nations, nor a sham parliament, such as the Assembly, is fitted for this task, which by its very nature can be satisfactorily performed only by an international court.

The Covenant of the League placed the Council, not the Permanent Court, at the center of the international organization because it conferred upon the League not only the task of maintaining peace within the community by settling disputes and by restricting the armament of the Member States, but also the duty of protecting them against aggression on the part of States non-Members of the League. This protection of Member States against aggression from the outside was all the more necessary because disarmament was set up as a main object of the League. The constitution of an international community can oblige a Member State to restrict its armament to a considerable extent only if this State can reckon upon efficacious help from the community in case it is attacked by another State not belonging to the community and therefore not obliged to disarm. This is possible only if the disarmament of the members is accompanied by an armament of the community, if an armed force is formed which is at the disposition of the central organ. Such a centralization of the executive power is not possible within an international-law community whose organization does not exceed the usual degree of centralization, and is therefore not provided by the Covenant of the League. If it is impossible to establish an armed force for the community of States—in other words, if it is not possible to establish a federal State—then the assistance rendered by the community to a victim of aggression from the outside can consist only of the obligation of the other members to defend the attacked State. Under such circumstances the duty of disarmament becomes contradictory to the necessity of defense against aggression. Nevertheless, the Covenant of the League puts the duty of disarmament in the foreground. Disarmament is to form the first duty of the Members of the League, placed immediately after Articles 1 to 7, which deal with the organization of the League.

The duty of a State which is a member of a universal in-

ternational community to defend another Member State
from attack by a non-member is very problematic, especially
if the international organization embraces many States
which have no common frontier, if these States have joined
in the first place for the purpose of maintaining peace
among each other, and if aside from this purpose they have
no political interest in common that might unite them
against the aggressor. It may be very difficult for a government to fulfill a duty to defend a Member State, to enter
into war against a State with which it is on good political
and economic terms, especially if the aggression is based on
grounds not entirely disapproved by the public opinion of
the State obliged to give its succor. The situation of Great
Britain and France in the conflict between Czechoslovakia
and Germany, a situation which led to the treaty of Munich,
is a characteristic example. Treaties obligating the contracting States to a joint war against third States are efficacious
only if concluded between States having more interests and
more important interests in common than those which form
the basis of an international community whose tendency is
to become as universal as possible. It is therefore not surprising that not only the provision of the League Covenant
concerning disarmament but also the provision concerning
mutual defense against aggression on the part of non-Member States (Article 10) has completely failed. The obvious
violation of the territorial integrity of a Member State, even
the total destruction of its political independence, as the
result of aggression on the part of a non-Member State was
not even made a subject of deliberation within the League;
and that despite the wording and the spirit of Article 10.*

---

* Article 10 of the Covenant of the League of Nations runs as follows:
"The Members of the League undertake to respect and preserve as against
external aggression the territorial integrity and existent political independ-

This article of the Covenant of the League of Nations obligates the Members of the League to preserve the territorial
integrity and political independence of all Members against
external aggression even if the aggressor is not a Member of
the League. The Council shall advise upon the means by
which this obligation shall be fulfilled. The Council may
advise the Members to resort to war against the aggressor.
The obligation of taking part in a military action may be
imposed upon the members of an international community,
not in order to defend a Member State against aggression on
the part of a non-member, but to react against aggression
undertaken by a Member State in violation of the constitution of the league. A military action against a Member State
which, contrary to the constitution, has attacked another
member of the league is, from the point of view of the ideology of the league, not "war" in the same sense as a military action against an aggressive non-Member State, but a
sanction, i.e., a reaction against a violation of law directed
at a delinquent member. The purpose of stipulating such

---

ence of all Members of the League. In case of any such aggression or in
case of any threat or danger of such aggression, the Council shall advise
upon the means by which this obligation shall be fulfilled." Aggression
on the part of non-Member States and aggression on the part of Member
States is not clearly distinguished in the text of this Article. By the term
"external" aggression certain enterprises against the territorial integrity
and the political independence of a Member State which come from the
very interior of the State itself—that is to say, revolutionary movements—
shall be excluded from the guarantee of Article 10. (Cf. Hans Kelsen,
*Legal Technique in International Law, A Textual Critique of the League
Covenant*, 1939, pp. 66 ff.) Since this Article refers to external aggression
in general, and not to aggression on the part of Member States, it has been
interpreted as establishing especially the obligation of preserving the
territorial integrity and political independence of all Members of the
League against aggression on the part of States which are not Members.
Aggression on the part of a Member State against another Member State
is the particular subject of Article 16, providing economic and military
sanctions against a delinquent Member State. With respect to this subject,
Article 10 and Article 16 are overlapping.

a sanction is to prevent war, to maintain peace within the league.

If the constitution of an international league obligates the members to submit all their disputes to the decision of a court, and, consequently, stipulates that no member must under any circumstances on its own initiative resort to war or reprisals against another member, the constitution must provide for the possibility of a member's refusing, in disregard of its obligation, to carry out an order or a decision of the court. In this case, too, a military action against the delinquent member may be necessary. In this case, too, the action has the character of a sanction and the purpose of stipulating such sanction is to maintain peace within the league.

The Covenant of the League of Nations, it is true, does not obligate the Members to submit all their disputes to the compulsory jurisdiction of a court, and it does not exclude completely war and reprisals in the relationship between the Members. But the Covenant forbids war between Members, at least under certain circumstances, and provides in Article 16 economic and military sanctions against a Member of the League which, in disregard of its obligations, resorts to war against another Member. It is a fact, the importance of which for the understanding of the function of an international community it is almost impossible to exaggerate, that the stipulations of Article 16 concerning sanctions against aggressive Member States have proved more efficacious than the provisions of Article 10 providing measures against non-Member States. As a matter of fact, the League of Nations, in spite of its complete failure in the cases of aggression on the part of non-Member States, has at least made certain efforts to fulfill its duty in the cases of illegal aggression undertaken by Member States against other Member States. This was the case in regard to Manchukuo, Abyssinia, and Finland.

The experiences of the League of Nations show that so long as the league does not comprise all States or, at least, all great Powers, it is necessary to make a clear distinction between the maintenance of peace between members and protection against aggression coming from the outside, and that it is hardly possible to fulfill the latter task by the specific means at the disposal of an international organization embracing many different States. It is a task with the fulfilling of which an international court has nothing to do. It is a function that lies beyond the possible activity of an international court, even beyond the power of an international union of States the organization of which does not exceed the usual degree of centralization. As long as it is impossible to constitute this union of States as a federal State, it seems to be more correct to limit its task to the maintenance of internal peace, and to leave protection against external aggression to political alliances between the Member States. These alliances may even have the character of permanent unions, much more centralized than the wider league. Such a closer union may be established especially by the United States of America and the British Empire, and must be established if these States accept the responsibility of political control of the vanquished countries. Such a closer union may be established by all the States of the American hemisphere, and must be established if, for one reason or another, the effects of this war should be the economic and political unification of the European continent or the Pacific area, as Prime Minister Churchill hinted in his speech on March 21, 1943, in the House of Commons.*

* *New York Times,* March 22, 1943.

10. A Permanent League for the Maintenance of Peace

THE CONSTITUTION of the wider league, leaving protection against aggression from the outside to regional organizations, should try to establish the strongest possible guarantee for maintaining peace within the league, that is, the obligation of the Member States to submit all their disputes without exception to the compulsory jurisdiction of an international court.

If the main organ of the international league for the maintenance of peace is an international court with compulsory jurisdiction, the constitution of the league must guarantee to this court the highest possible degree of independence and impartiality. The organization of the court becomes the central problem of the organization of peace. The Statute of the Permanent Court of International Justice which was established according to the Covenant of the League of Nations, in 1920, furnishes a useful starting point. This old court has no compulsory jurisdiction. The so-called "optional compulsory" jurisdiction provided for by Article 36 of the Statute is not compulsory in the true sense of the term, since the Members of the League are free to submit to this jurisdiction merely for a certain period of time and only with respect to certain disputes. The independence of the judges from their own governments, and the impartiality of the judicial decisions with respect to the States involved, can and must be assured in a more effective way than was assured by the Statute of the Permanent Court of International Justice, which concedes to the governments too much influence as regards the selection of the judges. If it should be possible to organize the new court in such a way that public opinion in the countries concerned would have faith in its independence and impartiality, we could reasonably hope that the governments concerned would ratify a treaty establishing such a court.

This hope has been supported by the above-mentioned speech of Prime Minister Churchill. He said that we must try to make the international organization to be established after this war "into a really effective League with all the strongest forces concerned woven into its texture, with a high court to adjust disputes and with forces, armed forces, national or international or both, held ready to enforce these decisions and prevent renewed aggression and preparation of future wars." Mr. Churchill, it is true, spoke in this context only of a European league. But we may assume that the British Government will accept the same principle for the universal community of which the European league will be only a regional group. The hope for such an international organization with an international court of compulsory jurisdiction at its center rests on more solid ground than the dream of a World State.

The Covenant of a Permanent League for the Maintenance of Peace (P.L.M.P.), presented in Annex I, is drafted according to the principles set forth in the foregoing paragraphs. Some provisions of the Covenant of the League of Nations (L.O.N.) and the Statute of the Permanent Court of International Justice (P.C.I.J.) are taken over. But in essential points the draft differs from both instruments.

The P.L.M.P. is open to any State which is willing to assume the obligations established by the Covenant. Hence a unilateral declaration on the part of the State which wishes to join the League suffices (Art. 1). No express admission by a majority vote of the members of the League (Art. 1, Sec. 2 of the Covenant of the L.O.N.) is necessary.

The organs of the P.L.M.P. are the Assembly, the Court, the Council, the Secretariat. The Court is the main organ (Art. 2). The Assembly (Art. 3) and the Council (Art. 27) are organized in the same way as the Assembly and the Council of the L.O.N. But their decisions require a simple majority of votes except where otherwise expressly provided in the Covenant, as, for instance, in Articles 38 and 39. In the draft a distinction is made between decisions of the Assembly binding upon the members and resolutions having no legal effect. Such resolutions may be the result of the discussion of matters affecting the international situation with the purpose of manifesting the opinion prevailing within the League. The Council is but a subsidiary agency of the Court. Its competence is determined by Articles 30, 35, and 36. The differentiation between permanent and non-permanent members of the Council is maintained. The question as to which States shall be permanent members of the Council is a political one. The draft suggests: The United States of America, Great Britain, Union of Socialist Soviet Republics, China.

The most important parts of the Covenant are the Articles concerning the organization of the Court.

Article 4 of the draft, concerning the general conditions that must be fulfilled by the judges, differs from the corresponding Article 2 of the Statute of the P.C.I.J., which runs as follows:

> The Permanent Court of International Justice shall be composed of a body of independent judges, elected regardless of their nationality from amongst persons of high moral character, who possess the qualifications required in their respective countries for appointment to the highest judicial offices, or are jurisconsults of recognized competence in international law.

Article 4 of the draft does not mention the independence of the judges. This character of the members of the Court is stipulated in a separate article (Art. 13).

Article 4 of the draft does not stipulate that the members of the Court shall be elected "regardless of their nationality." These words are from the point of view of legal technique superfluous if in the procedure of selecting the judges actually no regard is paid to the nationality of the judges. However, the nationality of the judges does play quite an important role in the Statute of the P.C.I.J. Thus Article 9 prescribes:

> At every election, the electors shall bear in mind that not only should all the persons appointed as members of the Court possess the qualifications required, but the whole body also should represent the main forms of civilization and the principal legal systems of the world.

Article 10 stipulates:

> Those candidates who obtain an absolute majority of votes in the Assembly and in the Council shall be considered as elected. In the event of more than one national of the same Member of the League being elected by the votes of both the Assembly and the Council, the eldest of these only shall be considered as elected.

And Article 31 provides for so-called national judges:

> Judges of the nationality of each of the contesting parties shall retain their right to sit in the case before the Court. If the Court includes upon the Bench a judge of the nationality of one of the parties, the other party may choose a person to sit as judge. Such person shall be chosen preferably from among those persons who have been nominated as candidates as provided in Articles 4 and 5.

If the Court includes upon the Bench no judge of the nationality of the contesting parties, each of these parties may proceed to select a judge as provided in the preceding paragraph.

The draft does not adopt these provisions.

Finally, Article 4 of the draft differs from Article 2 of the Statute of the P.C.I.J. in that the alternative requirement "qualification for appointment to the highest judicial office" has been dropped. It is suggested that the Court shall be composed of seventeen members (Art. 4), whereas the P.C. I.J. is composed of fifteen members. The greater number of judges is justified by the fact that, according to Article 16, Sec. 2 of the draft, judges who are of the nationality of the contesting parties are excluded from the decision of any case in which their home State is one of the contesting parties. It is quite possible, however, that even the number of seventeen judges will not suffice when the number of cases to be decided by the Court increases because of the compulsory character of its jurisdiction. Consequently Article 39, Sec. 2, provides that amendments concerning only the number of the judges shall take effect when voted by the Assembly on a simple majority. It is advisable to provide for the possibility of deciding cases by special Chambers of five or seven judges (Art. 24, Sec. 2).

According to the Statute of the P.C.I.J. the judges are appointed for nine years only; they are elected by the Assembly and Council of the L.O.N. from a list of candidates nominated by the so-called "national groups." A "national group" is a group of four persons, at the most, appointed by the respective governments of the States. Each national group nominates not more than four persons, not more than two of them of their own nationality. Article 6 of the Statute of the P.C.I.J. stipulates:

Before making these nominations, each national group is recommended to consult its Highest Court of Justice, its Legal Faculties and Schools of Law, and its National Academies and national sections of International Academies devoted to the study of law.

The Secretary General of the L.O.N. prepares an alphabetical list of all the persons thus nominated by the national groups. It is from this list that the members of the P.C.I.J. are elected by the Assembly and the Council of the L.O.N. In the Assembly as well as in the Council, the States are represented by members of their governments or by delegates appointed by their governments. Thus the influence of the governments on the selection of the judges is decisive. The judge remains, during his tenure, a citizen of his State and consequently owes allegiance to his government. This is all the more critical as re-election of a judge is possible and even desirable in order to conserve for the Court his valuable experience.

The annexed draft tries to strengthen the independence of the judges from their governments by the following measures: (1) The judges are appointed for life, but they may be retired by the Court if they become physically or mentally unable to exercise their function (Art. 17, Sec. 2). The draft contains, however, an alternative provision according to which a judge is obliged to retire when he has finished his seventieth year. The provision of Article 17, Sec. 3, corresponds to that of Article 18 of the Statute of the P.C.I.J. (2) The draft eliminates the national groups and grants to the institutions concerned with the administration and teaching of law in the member States—namely, their supreme courts, legal faculties, etc., which are more or less independent from their governments—a direct influence on the selection of the judges (Art. 6-12). The appointment of the judges is different as regards the first establishment of the Court and the later filling of vacancies. The first establishment of the Court is composed of two different procedures. Nine judges are elected directly by the above mentioned institutions of the member States (Art. 10). These judges are nominated by the institutions of States of which the candidates are not nationals. This is effected by the stipulation (Art. 8) that the first part of the list of candidates shall contain the names of persons nominated by institutions which are not of the nationality of the candidates, and that the first nine persons registered in this part of the list shall be considered appointed judges of the Court. The chance of a person to become one of these nine judges is determined in the first place by the number of States whose institutions have nominated the person; in the second place, by the number of institutions which have nominated the person. Eight judges are elected by the Assembly from that part of the list of candidates which contains the names of persons nominated by institutions of their own States (Art. 9). The later filling of vacancies takes place according to the principle of co-optation by the Court and is combined with election by the Assembly. (3) Article 14 of the draft stipulates that the citizenship of the judges and the allegiance to their governments is suspended during their function. In order to compensate the disadvantages of temporary statelessness, it is provided that the document certifying the membership in the Court is to be recognized as a diplomatic passport.

In order to guarantee the highest possible degree of impartiality, the draft differs essentially from the Statute of the P.C.I.J. Article 31 of the Statute (quoted above), providing for national judges, obviously presupposes that the impi ;iality of a judge is impaired when one of the contesting parties is of his own nationality. The Statute tries to neutralize the partiality of that judge by the partiality of another judge who may be of the nationality of the other party. This is not an ideal solution of the problem. The opposite solution seems to be a better guarantee of judicial impartiality: no judge should be allowed to participate in the decision of any case in which his home State is one of the contesting parties. His home State is the State whose citizen he was before he was appointed member of the Court and whose citizen he will be again after he ceases to be a member of the Court, since his citizenship is only suspended during this period of time. This is the solution suggested by Article 16, Sec. 2.

The compulsory jurisdiction of the Court is stipulated by Articles 31-37. The draft does not prescribe, but it does not exclude a procedure of conciliation. According to Article 31, the dispute must be settled by judicial decision if one party submits it to the Court; consequently, a procedure of conciliation is possible only if both parties agree upon it. Such an agreement is compatible with the Covenant. In the event that the parties agree to have recourse to conciliation, Article 31 of the Covenant is applicable only if conciliation fails to succeed.

Article 38 of the draft is an attempt to improve Article 19 of the Covenant of the L.O.N. The latter Article runs as follows:

> The Assembly may from time to time advise the reconsideration by Members of the League of treaties which have become inapplicable and the consideration of international conditions whose continuance might endanger the peace of 'ie world.

It is easy to understand why this Article has never been applied. It was, from the very beginning, inapplicable because the decision of the Assembly could be reached only by unanimous vote, and even if reached, would have had no legal effect at all. It was not worthwhile to bring about a unanimous decision of the Assembly to the effect only of giving not-binding advice to the Members. Article 38 of the draft tries to establish a kind of negative legislation. The Assembly is not empowered to enact positive norms binding upon the members; it can only invalidate international treaties that endanger the peace. But this Article is not at all essential.

Article 39, Sec. 1, of the draft, concerning amendments to the Covenant, corresponds, in principle, to Article 26 of the Covenant of the L.O.N. by taking into account the amendment to this Article voted in 1921. A remarkable difference exists, however, in that, according to Article 39 of the draft, no ratification of the decision of the Assembly on the part of the governments is required, and that a member of the League which has voted against the amendment cannot escape its binding force by withdrawing from the League, as it is provided by the express provisions of Article 26, Sec. 2, of the Covenant of the L.O.N.

The Covenant of the P.L.M.P., as drafted in the Annex, does not confer upon the members the right of secession, as the Covenant of the L.O.N. does in its Article 1, Sec. 3, and Article 26, Sec. 2. Nor does the Covenant of the P.L.M.P. stipulate the expulsion of a member as a sanction against a violation of the Covenant, as the Covenant of the L.O.N. does in Article 16, Sec. 4. The possibility of withdrawing from the League is practically nothing else but the possibility of getting rid of the obligation not to resort to war against a Member of the League. The difference between the L.O.N. and the P.L.M.P. in this point consists, practically, only in the character of the reaction against the aggressor. If a Member of the L.O.N. has withdrawn from the League in order to be in a situation to attack a Member of the League without violating the Covenant, Article 10 of the Covenant of the L.O.N. has to be applied. This means that the reaction of the League against the aggressor has the character of a war or reprisals. According to the draft covenant of the P.L.M.P., the aggression is always a violation of the Covenant, and the reaction of the P.L.M.P. always a sanction directed against a violator of the Covenant. An international confederacy of States, the members of which have no right of secession, is not without precedent. The Briand-Kellogg Pact furnishes an important example. It does not confer upon the contracting parties the legal possibility of denouncing the treaty unilaterally, which amounts to the same thing as withdrawing of a Member State by a one-sided declaration from the legal community constituted by the treaty.

Another essential difference between the L.O.N. and the P.L.M.P. is to be noted in that the function of the latter is restricted to the maintenance of peace within the community by settling all the disputes between the members through judicial decisions. Hence no obligation of mutual protection against aggression from the outside (Art. 10 of the Covenant of the L.O.N.) is imposed upon the members; and, consequently, no obligation of disarmament of the members (Art. 8 and 9 of the Covenant of the L.O.N.) is stipulated. Disarmament of the vanquished States shall be stipulated by the peace treaties, from which the Covenant of the P.L.M.P. must be separated. The great mistake which was committed by making the Covenant of the L.O.N. part

of the Peace Treaties of 1920 is to be avoided.* The P.L.
M.P. shall be a legal, not a political community.

*   *   *

If it were possible to obtain, for a treaty such as that suggested, the ratification of the United States, Great Britain,
China, and the Soviet Union, it would be almost certain that
these great Powers would conscientiously respect the stipulations of the treaty and, if ordered by the Court or the
Council, execute the judicial decisions against any member
of the League which would dare to violate the Covenant
and, in particular, to refuse obedience to the Court. The
very fact that the four great Powers were to be considered
the guarantors of the Covenant would render any serious
violation of it unlikely.

The objection that such a Covenant would establish
hegemony of the four guarantors over the other members
of the League is not quite justifiable. So long as the guarantors themselves respect the Covenant, their "hegemony"
is nothing more than the enforcement of the law. They are
the power "behind the law" for which those realists who
conceive of the law as a mere ideology of force might en-
quire. From such a realistic point of view, the true function
of the Covenant may be to secure the exercise by the great
Powers of their inevitable preponderance for no other purpose and in no other form than that of law. To provide for
the possibility that the guarantors themselves may cease to
obey the law is impossible, not only with respect to the suggested treaty, but also with respect to any legal order what-

* Cf. Hans Kelsen, "The Separation of the Covenant of the League of
Nations from the Peace Treaties," *The World Crisis, Symposium of Studies
Published on the Occasion of the Tenth Anniversary of the Graduate
Institute of International Studies, Geneva* (1938), pp. 133-159.

ever, since no legal order can solve the problem of *quis custodiet custodes.*

In his speech of May 24, 1944, Prime Minister Churchill told Commons: "We intend to set up a world order and an organization equipped with all necessary attributes of power in order to prevent future wars or the planning of them in advance by restless and ambitious Nations." His suggested "world organization," he said, would embody much of the structure of the League of Nations, but this time it must bristle with "overwhelming military power." * The more effective the power conferred upon the international organization, the more guarantees which must be given by its constitution that this power will be exercised only for the maintenance of the law; and the only serious guarantee for the legal exercise of power is the provision that the armed forces at the disposal of the League—whether a true international police force or the armed forces of one or several member States—is to be employed not at the order of a political body but in execution of the decision of a court.

* *New York Times*, May 25, 1944.

Part II

PEACE GUARANTEED BY INDIVIDUAL
RESPONSIBILITY FOR VIOLATIONS
OF INTERNATIONAL LAW

11. Individual responsibility of the authors of war

ONE OF THE MOST EFFECTIVE means to prevent war and to guarantee international peace is the enactment of rules establishing individual responsibility of the persons who as members of government have violated international law by resorting to or provoking war.* It is a fundamental principle of general international law that war is permitted only as a reaction against a wrong suffered—that is to say, as a sanction—and that any war which has not this character is a delict, i.e., a violation of international law. This is the substance of the principle of *bellum justum* (just war). † Almost all the States are contracting parties to the Briand-Kellogg Pact, by which war as a means of national policy is outlawed. Resorting to war may be a delict not only according to general international law or according to the Briand-Kellogg Pact, but also according to a special treaty concluded by two States, such as a non-aggression pact.

There can be no doubt that Germany by resorting to war

* Cf. Hans Kelsen, "Collective and Individual Responsibility in International Law with Particular Regard to the Punishment of War Criminals," *California Law Review* (1943), Vol. 31, pp. 530 ff.

† Most of the writers on international law do not recognize the principle of just war as a rule of positive law. In Hans Kelsen, *Law and Peace in International Relations* (1942), pp. 34 ff., the main arguments *pro* and *contra* this view are presented.

against Poland and Soviet Russia, Italy by resorting to war against France, and Japan by resorting to war against China and the United States have violated not only the *bellum justum* principle of general international law but also the Briand-Kellogg Pact, to which the Axis Powers are contracting parties. Moreover, Germany by resorting to war against Poland and Soviet Russia has violated the non-aggression pacts concluded with these States. The requirement to punish the war criminals is, or ought to be, above all, the requirement to punish the authors of the second World War, the persons morally responsible for one of the greatest crimes in the history of mankind.

To punish the authors of a war means making certain individuals responsible by punishing them for acts committed by themselves, at their command, or with their authorization. This does not mean to punish a State as such, that is, a State as a body corporate. Most writers maintain that the sanctions which international law provides against States as such, namely, reprisals and war, are not punishments in the sense of criminal law. The difference, however, between the specific sanctions of international law directed against States and the sanctions of criminal law directed against individuals is not clearly manifest. Punishment is forcible deprivation of life, freedom, or property for the purpose of retribution or prevention. This definition applies to the specific sanctions of international law, war and reprisals, as well. That the perpetrator must have a guilty mind, that he must have brought about the harmful effect of his conduct willfully and maliciously or with culpable negligence, does not, as is sometimes maintained, exclude "punishment" of States. The rule of *mens rea* (guilty mind) is not without exceptions. That an individual is to be punished although he has not acted willfully and maliciously or with culpable negligence, so-called "absolute liability," is not completely excluded, even in modern criminal law. Moreover, according to some writers, a State is responsible for its acts only if they are committed by its organs willfully and maliciously or with culpable negligence.* The opinion that the State as a body corporate cannot have a guilty mind because it has no psychic functions is not conclusive. The State acts only through individuals; acts of State are acts performed by individuals in their capacity as organs of the State and therefore acts imputed to the State. If only acts committed by the organs of the State "willfully and maliciously or with culpable negligence" are imputable as delicts to the State, it is quite possible to say that the State must have a "guilty mind" in order to be made responsible for a delict. If it is possible to impute physical acts performed by individuals to the State although the State has no physical body, it must be possible to impute psychic acts to the State, although the State has no soul. Imputation to the State is a juristic construction, not a description of natural reality.

In order to refute the prevailing doctrine *societas delinquere non potest* (a corporation cannot commit a crime) and to prove that States can incur criminal responsibility, it is not necessary to make the hopeless attempt to demonstrate that the State as a juristic person is not a legal fiction but a real being, a super-individual organism, and the like.† The decisive question is not whether the State is a legal fiction or a real thing but whether the sanctions which are to be directed against the State as such, that is, war and reprisals, can be interpreted as "punishment." Such an inter-

* Cf. L. Oppenheim, *International Law* (5th Ed., 1937), Vol. I, p. 227.
† For instance: Vespasian V. Pella, "De l'influence d'une juridiction criminelle internationale," *Revue Internationale de Droit pénal* (1926), Vol. 3, pp. 391 ff.

pretation is certainly possible. There is, however, an important difference between the sanctions international law provides against States and the sanctions provided for by modern criminal law.

The difference consists in the fact that punishment—at least in modern criminal law—implies individual responsibility, whereas the specific sanctions of international law imply collective responsibility. Punishment is directed against the individual who, by his own conduct, has violated the law, has personally committed the crime; thus criminal law directs its sanctions against a precisely determined individual as that individual who by his own conduct has performed the act which constitutes the crime. Criminal law establishes individual responsibility. The specific sanctions of international law, reprisals and war, are not directed against the individual whose conduct constitutes the violation of international law. Reprisals and war are directed against the State as such, and that means against the subjects of the State, against individuals who have not committed the delict or have not had the ability to prevent it. The individuals against whom reprisals and war are directed are the subjects of the State whose organ has violated international law. International law answers the question "Against whom are the sanctions to be directed?" not, as national criminal law does, by designating a certain human being individually, but by designating a certain group of individuals, individuals who stand in a certain legal relation to the individual who, by his own conduct, has performed the act constituting the delict—namely, the individuals who are the subjects of the State whose organ has committed the delict. This is the scheme for collective responsibility. The statement that according to international law the State is responsible for its acts means that the subjects of the State are collectively responsible for the acts of the organs of the State; and the statement that international law imposes duties on States and not on individuals means, in the first place, that the specific sanctions of international law, reprisals and war, are applied in recognition of collective, not individual, responsibility.

12. Individual responsibility established by general international law

THE ESTABLISHMENT of collective responsibility by international law, however, constitutes a rule with important exceptions. There are norms of general international law by which the person against whom a sanction is to be directed is individually determined as the person who, by his own conduct, has violated international law. These norms establish individual responsibility. Such a norm of general international law is the rule forbidding piracy. The delict, committed on the open sea, is directly determined by general international law, which authorizes the States to attack, seize, and punish the pirate. International law does not authorize the States to resort to reprisals or war against the State whose subject or vessel has committed acts of piracy. It authorizes the States to execute sanctions only against the individuals who committed acts of piracy. The norm of general international law conferring upon States the legal power to prosecute pirates is a restriction of another rule of general international law, namely, the rule establishing the freedom of the open sea. If international law did not confer upon the States the right to attack, seize, and punish the pirate, these acts would be violations of the principle of the freedom of the open sea. Only by a norm of general international law can the norm establishing the freedom of the open sea be restricted. The fact that the specification of the punishment is left to national law, and the trial of the pirate to national courts, does not deprive the delict and the sanction of their international character. A State which in its criminal law attaches to piracy a certain punishment, and punishes a pirate through its courts executes international law and functions as an organ of the international community, just as a State which resorts to reprisals against another State which has violated the former's right enforces international law. Reprisals are international sanctions because their legal basis is international law, although they are executed by organs of the injured State. The same is true of the punishment of pirates by national courts; a court is an organ of the State just as are its administrative agencies or its armed force through which the State exercises reprisals. The rule of general international law forbidding piracy is a rule of international criminal law, imposing a legal duty directly upon individuals and establishing individual responsibility. Consequently, the doctrine that international law by its very nature cannot oblige individuals, and hence cannot have the character of criminal law, is not correct.

Other norms of general international law by which individuals are directly obligated and individual responsibility is established are the rules concerning breach of blockade and carriage of contraband. In these cases general international law not only directly determines the individual against whom a sanction is to be directed, but also specifies the sanction, which is the confiscation of the vessel and the cargo. The national prize courts, by deciding cases of blockade and contraband, execute not only national, but also international law, and hence function as organs not only of national but also of international law. Whether the sanction has in these cases the character of "punishment," or more resembles civil execution, is of no importance. It is decisive that a rule of general international law establishes individual responsibility, that is, the responsibility of the owner of the vessel and the cargo who is guilty of breach of blockade or carriage of contraband.

Another example of direct obligation of individuals and individual responsibility established by general international law is the rule concerning specific acts of illegitimate warfare, sometimes characterized as "war crimes." This is the rule of general international law according to which private individuals, not belonging to the armed forces of the enemy, who take up arms against the armed forces of the occupant State may be considered by the latter as criminals. International law confers upon the occupant State the right to punish such individuals for acts of illegitimate warfare, even if their acts are not crimes according to the law of their country and although the occupant State is, as a rule, obliged to apply to the inhabitants of the occupied country their own law. These acts are forbidden directly by international law. The military court, by punishing the acts, executes international law even if it applies at the same time norms of its own military law. The legal basis of the trial is international law, which establishes the individual responsibility of the person committing the act of illegitimate warfare. If it must be admitted that international law gives the occupant State the right to punish inhabitants of the occupied territory for acts of illegitimate warfare, then it is inconsistent to say that international law, as a law between States only, cannot prohibit private individuals from taking up arms and committing hostilities against the enemy. For, to "prohibit" legally a certain conduct means nothing else than to attach to that conduct a sanction; and international law, by giving the occupant State "the right" to punish acts of illegitimate warfare, prohibits these acts, which may not be prohibited by the national law of the perpetrators.

Violations of international law may be committed by acts of private persons, acts committed in the territory of one State but injurious to another State; for instance, certain individuals may prepare an armed expedition in the territory of State A against State B. These acts are not acts of State, but acts for which the State in whose territory the acts have been committed is responsible insofar as the State is obliged to prevent these acts and, if prevention is not possible, to punish the delinquents and compel them to pay damages. These are cases of so-called vicarious responsibility of the State for acts that are not its own acts. By punishing the perpetrators, the State executes international law, even if national law is also applied to the delinquents. If national law attaches sanctions to the acts concerned, it does so in execution of international law. Consequently, one can say that international law imposes upon individuals the obligation to abstain from acts injurious to other States, and that international law in these cases also establishes individual responsibility.

13. Individual responsibility established by particular international law

IT STANDS TO REASON that individual responsibility for violations of international law can be established by particular international law, for instance, by an international treaty. An example is the abortive treaty relating to the use of submarines concluded at Washington on February 6, 1922. Article 3 of this treaty states that any person in the service of any State who shall violate any rule of this treaty relative to the attack, capture, or destruction of commercial ships, whether or not he is under order of a governmental superior,

> ...shall be deemed to have violated the laws of war and shall be liable to trial and punishment as if for an act of piracy and may be brought to trial before the civil or military authorities of any Power within the jurisdiction of which he may be found.

According to general international law, a person who, in the service of a State, has violated a rule of international law is not responsible. But by an international treaty, such persons can be made responsible. The treaty of Washington is problematical insofar as it does not restrict its validity to the contracting States. As we shall see later, an individual who, in his capacity as an organ of a State, has violated international law can be made responsible for such an act of State by another State only with the consent of his home State. The attempt to overcome this difficulty by using the fiction that violation of the norms of the Treaty of Washington is to be considered as piracy, for which general international law establishes individual responsibility, is vain, since a violation of the Treaty of Washington is not piracy. Piracy cannot be an act of State, whereas the delicts determined by the Washington Treaty may be and mostly are acts of State.

The International Convention for the Protection of Submarine Telegraph Cables, signed at Paris on March 14, 1884, is also an example of a rule of international law directly obligating individuals and establishing individual responsibility. Article II of the Convention stipulates:

> The breaking or injury of a submarine cable, done willfully or through culpable negligence, and resulting in the total or partial interruption or embarrassment of tele-

graphic communication, shall be a punishable offense, but the punishment inflicted shall be no bar to a civil action for damages.

A norm of international law directly defines a delict and attaches criminal as well as civil sanctions to an act committed by an individual determined by this norm. The Convention obliges the States to specify by their national law the sanctions (punishment and civil execution) provided for by Article II, and obliges the State to which the vessel belongs and on board which the delict defined in Article II was committed, to execute the sanctions. The national courts, by punishing an individual for the breaking or injury of a submarine cable or by ordering reparation of the damage caused by the delict, execute international law even if they apply their national law at the same time. The individuals concerned are obliged by international law to abstain from a delict determined by international law, even if their national law also requires the same conduct. Their criminal, as well as their civil, responsibility is directly established by international law, in addition to its establishment by national law. This interpretation is correct even if the courts are obliged by the constitution of their State to apply only national law so that a so-called transformation of a norm of international into national law is necessary in order to be executed within the State. The necessity of transforming international into national law, imposed by a national constitution, cannot alter the fact that the enactment of the statute by which the transformation is carried out and its application by the courts is an execution of international law, the fulfillment of an international obligation of the State, whose legislative and judicial organs function here as organs of international law.

14. Individual responsibility for acts of State

PUBLIC OPINION DEMANDS that the authors of the present
war, the individuals who are morally responsible for it, the
persons who have, as organs of the States, in disregard of
general or particular international law, resorted to or provoked this war shall be made legally responsible by the injured States. If this demand is to be met in conformity with
international law, it is necessary to take into consideration
that the acts for which the guilty persons are to be punished
are acts of State, that is, according to general international
law, acts of the government, or performed at the government's command, or with its authorization.

The legal meaning of the statement that an act is an act
of State is that this act is to be imputed to the State, not to
the individual who has performed the act. If an act performed by an individual—and all acts of State are performed
by individuals—must be imputed to the State, the latter is
responsible for this act; and that, so far as general international law is concerned, means that the State injured by this
act is authorized to resort to war or reprisals against the
State whose act constitutes the violation of law. These sanctions, as pointed out, imply collective, not individual responsibility. If an act is imputed to the State and not to the
individual who has performed it, the individual, according
to general international law, cannot be made responsible
for this act by another State without the consent of the State
whose act is concerned. As far as the relationship of the State
to its own agents or subjects is concerned, national law
comes into consideration. And in national law the same
principle prevails: an individual is not responsible for his
act if it is an act of State, i.e., if the act is not imputable to

the individual but only to the State.* The other State, injured by such an act, can, without violating international law, make only the State whose act constitutes the violation of international law responsible for the act, and the injured State may resort to reprisals or war against the responsible State. But prosecution of an individual by a court of the injured State for an act which, according to international law, is the act of another State, amounts to exercising jurisdiction over another State; and this is a violation of the rule of general international law that no State is subject to the jurisdiction of another State. Since the legal existence of a State manifests itself only in acts of individuals which, according to international law, are acts of State, the generally accepted rule that no State can claim jurisdiction over another State means that no State can claim civil or criminal jurisdiction over the act of another State. The immunity

---

* This rule seems to be not without exceptions. An individual who in his capacity as organ of the State has performed an illegal act may be made responsible for it. Thus, according to the law of some States, a Cabinet minister, and even the Head of State, may be accused and punished for having violated the constitution by one of his acts. But when the act is declared by the competent authority to be illegal with regard to the State's own law, it ceases to be an act of State—that is to say, the act can no longer be imputed to the State, whether it be annullable or not. To impute to the State an act that by the competent authority is declared to be illegal with regard to the State's own law is incompatible with the fact that the State, conceived of as an acting person, is but the personification of this law, i.e., the national legal order (or, what amounts to the same, the personification of the community constituted by this legal order). Within national law an act performed by an individual can be imputed to the State only on the basis of a legal rule; imputation of an act to the State is subsumption of the act under a specific rule of law; and an individual can be considered as organ of the State only insofar as he performs acts imputable to the State. If an act is considered to be illegal with regard to the law of the State, it is hardly possible to interpret this act as act of State; and within national law the predicate "act of State" is a specific interpretation of an act performed by an individual. The State can do no wrong with regard to its own law, although the State can well do wrong with regard to international law.

from the jurisdiction of another State is not, as this principle is usually formulated, attached to the very "person" of the State—the "person" of the State is a juristic construction—but to the acts of the State as the acts performed by the government, at its command, or with its authorization. The generally recognized principle that the courts of a State are not competent with regard to another State means that the courts of a State are not competent with regard to the acts of another State. Consequently, this principle applies not only where the defendant is expressly designated as "State X" or the "person" of State X, but also where the defendant is an individual sued personally for an act performed by him as an act of State X.* The collective responsibility of a State for its own acts excludes, according to general international law, the individual responsibility of the person who, as a member of the government, at the command or with the authorization of the government, has performed the act. † This is a consequence of the immunity of

---

* In the Report adopted by the Committee of Experts for the Progressive Codification of International Law at its third session, March-April, 1927, Rapporteur Matsuda (Publications of the League of Nations, Legal, 1927, V. 9 in *American Journal of International Law*, 1928, Vol. 22, Supp., p. 125), it is said: "The inability of courts to exercise jurisdiction in regard to a sovereign act of a foreign government . . . should apply where the defendant is sued personally for acts done by him in his capacity as a public official—though he no longer retains that capacity at the time of the proceedings—or under powers conferred upon him by a foreign State."

† In the famous case of McLeod (member of a British force sent in 1837 into the territory of the United States for the purpose of capturing the *Caroline*, arrested in 1840 in the State of New York, and indicted for the killing of an American citizen on the occasion of the capture of the *Caroline*), Mr. Webster, Secretary of State, wrote Mr. Crittenden, Attorney General, March 15, 1841: "All that is intended to be said at present is, that, since the attack on the *Caroline* is avowed as a national act, which may justify reprisals, or even general war, if the Government of the United States, in the judgment which it shall form of the transaction and of its own duty, should see fit so to decide, yet that it raises a question entirely public and political, a question between independent nations; and that

the State from the jurisdiction of another State. This rule is not without exceptions, but any exception must be based on a special rule of customary or conventional international law restricting the former *

In this respect there exists no difference between the Head of a State and the other State officials. † That the Head of a State is not individually responsible to another State for acts performed by him in his capacity as organ of his State is not due to the personal privilege of exemption from the criminal and civil jurisdiction of another State granted to Heads of State by general international law. Non-responsibility of the Head of State for his acts of State is the consequence of the rule of international law that no State can claim jurisdiction, exercised by its courts, over acts of another State. The personal privilege of exemption from criminal and civil jurisdiction of another State granted by international law to Heads of State refers, in the first place,

---

individuals connected in it cannot be arrested and tried before the ordinary tribunals, as for the violation of municipal law. If the attack on the *Caroline* was unjustifiable, as this Government has asserted, the law which has been violated is the law of nations; and the redress which is to be sought is the redress authorized, in such cases, by the provisions of that code." Cf. John Basset Moore, *A Digest of International Law* (1906). Vol. II, Sec. 179. Cf. further: *Woerterbuch des Voelkerrechts und der Diplomatie*, Herausgegeben von Karl Strupp (1925), Vol. II. p. 2: "The State is responsible for the acts of all its organs, but the organs are not responsible at all insofar as they act in their capacity as organs of the State."

* See *infra*, pp. 98 ff.

† In the memorandum of the American members of the Commission on Responsibilities established at the close of the first World War by the Preliminary Peace Conference (*American Journal of International Law*, 1920, Vol. 14. p. 136), it is said that "Proceedings ... against an individual in office" are "in effect" proceedings "against the State." The American members of the Commission on Responsibilities advanced this argument to justify their opposition against the intention to bring Wilhelm II to justice before an international tribunal. They refused to subject a Chief of State "to a degree of responsibility hitherto unknown to municipal or international law."

not to acts of State performed by the Head of a State, but rather to acts committed abroad by the Head of a State in his capacity as a private person. Consequently, the same privilege can be and is granted by international law to the wife of the Head of a State who may never perform an act of State. The personal privilege of exterritoriality must be granted to a Head of a State only as long as he is actually in office, not after he has been deposed or has abdicated, or his office has expired. For his act of State, however, he is individually not responsible to another State, even after his deposition, abdication, or expiration of office, since the act was performed when he was still in office; otherwise the act could not have been an act of State. Non-responsibility of the Head of a State for his acts of State, based on the rule that no State can claim jurisdiction over the acts of another State, works also in the case where the Head of a State has fallen into his enemies' hands as prisoner of war, even if his personal privilege of exterritoriality does not work because it is limited to the time of peace and does not apply in time of war. There is no sufficient reason to assume that the rule of general customary law under which no State can claim jurisdiction over the acts of another State is suspended by the outbreak of war, and consequently that it is not applicable to the relationship between belligerents.*

Exclusion of individual responsibility constitutes the difference which exists between the State's collective responsibility for its own acts, its "original" responsibility, and the State's collective responsibility for acts other than its own, namely, certain violations of international law committed by individuals not at the command or with the authorization of the government—the State's "vicarious" responsibility. Vicarious responsibility of the State does not exclude

* See *infra*, p. 78.

the individual responsibility of the persons who have performed the acts constituting the violation of international law; on the contrary, their individual responsibility is implied by the responsibility of the State insofar as the latter is obliged by international law to punish these individuals and to compel them to repair the illegally caused damage.

If individuals are to be punished for acts which they have performed as acts of State, by a court of another State, or by an international court, as a rule the legal basis of the trial must be an international treaty concluded with the State whose acts are to be punished. By such treaty the jurisdiction over these individuals would be conferred upon the national or international court. If that court is a national court, then it functions, at least indirectly, as an international court. It is national only with respect to its composition, insofar as the judges are appointed by one government only; it is international, however, with respect to the legal basis of its jurisdiction.

The law of a State does not contain norms that attach sanctions to acts of other States which violate international law. Resorting to war in disregard of a rule of general or particular international law is a violation of international law but is not a violation of national criminal law, as are violations of the rules of international law which regulate the conduct of war. The substantive law applied by a court competent to punish individuals for the crime of having made war can be international law only. Hence the international treaty mentioned in the preceding paragraph must not only determine the delict but also the punishment, or must authorize the court to fix the punishment which it considers to be adequate. If a national court is authorized and if the national constitution obliges the courts to apply only norms created by the legislative (or other law-making) organ of the State, the norms of international law authorizing the State to punish individuals who, as organs of another State, have violated international law must be transformed into norms of the national law of the State to the jurisdiction of which these individuals are subjected by the treaty. An international treaty authorizing a court to punish individuals for acts they have performed as acts of their State constitutes a norm of international criminal law with retroactive force, if the acts at the moment when they were committed were not crimes for which the individual perpetrators were responsible. There is no rule of general customary international law forbidding the enactment of norms with retroactive force, so-called *ex post facto* laws. But some State constitutions forbid that type of regulations expressly, and it is a principle of criminal law recognized by most of the civilized nations that no punishment must be attached to an act which was not legally punishable at the moment of its performance. Some writers, abandoning the positivist view, maintain that not only custom and treaties but also the general principles of law are to be considered as sources of international law. This doctrine is very questionable and, even if accepted, does not exclude an international treaty authorizing a court to punish the persons morally responsible for the second World War. The principle forbidding the enactment of norms with retroactive force as a rule of positive national law is not without many exceptions. Its basis is the moral idea that it is not just to make an individual responsible for an act if he, when performing the act, did not and could not know that his act constituted a wrong. If, however, the act was at the moment of its performance morally, although not legally wrong, a law attaching *ex post facto* a sanction to the act is retroactive only from a legal, not from a moral point of view. Such a law is not contrary to the moral idea which is at the basis of the principle in question. This is in particular true of an international treaty by which individuals are made responsible for having violated, in their capacity as organs of a State, international law. Morally they were responsible for the violation of international law at the moment when they performed the acts constituting a wrong not only from a moral but also from a legal point of view. The treaty only transforms their moral into a legal responsibility. The principle forbidding *ex post facto* laws is, in all reason, not applicable to such a treaty.

15. The question of war guilt in the first and in the second World War

IN ITS REPORT presented to the Preliminary Peace Conference on March 29, 1919, the Commission on the Responsibility of the Authors of the War and Enforcement of Penalties distinguished "two classes of culpable acts: (a) Acts which provoked the world war and accompanied its inception; (b) Violations of the laws and customs of war and the laws of humanity." The Commission advised that the acts which provoked the war should not be charged against their authors and made the subject of proceedings before a tribunal.* Nevertheless, the Peace Treaty of Versailles stipulated in Article 227:

> The Allied and Associated Powers publicly arraign William II of Hohenzollern, formerly German Emperor, for a supreme offence against international morality and the sanctity of treaties. A special tribunal will be constituted to try the accused, thereby assuring him the guaran-

* *American Journal of International Law* (1920), Vol. 14, pp. 95 ff., 117 ff.

tees essential to the right of defence. It will be composed of five judges, one appointed by each of the following Powers; namely, the United States of America, Great Britain, France, Italy, and Japan.

The formula "for a supreme offence against international morality and the sanctity of treaties" is insincere and inconsistent. The true reason for demanding the ex-Kaiser's submission to a criminal court was that he was considered the main author of the war, and resorting to this war was considered a crime. Article 227 speaks of "an offence against international morality" in order to avoid speaking of a violation of international law. But if a legal norm—one established by an international treaty—attaches punishment to an offense of morality, a punishment to be inflicted upon the offender by a court, the offense assumes *ex post facto* the character of a violation of law. Article 227 speaks also of an offense against the "sanctity of treaties." This means a violation of treaties, which is a delict according to international law.

The main reasons for the negative advice of the Commission on Responsibilities were, in the first place, that, according to the opinion of the Commission, "a war of aggression may not be considered as an act directly contrary to positive law, or one which can be successfully brought before a tribunal such as the Commission is authorized to consider under its terms of reference"; in the second place, that "any inquiry into the authorship of the war must, to be exhaustive, extend over events that have happened during many years in different European countries, and must raise many difficult and complex problems which might be more fitly investigated by historians and statesmen than by a tribunal appropriate to the trial of offenders against the laws and customs of war."

The validity of the proposition that a war of aggression is not an act contrary to positive law is, at least, very doubtful. The principle of *bellum justum* is considered, it is true, not by many but by some outstanding authors as a rule of positive international law. It is, however, precisely the Peace Treaty of Versailles and the other Peace Treaties of 1919-20 which confirm the doctrine of just war.

The Peace Treaties did not oblige the vanquished States to pay a war indemnity, but rather to make reparation. The obligation of reparation is considered to be a consequence attached by general international law to a violation of law. That the Peace Treaties substitute the obligation of reparation, established by general international law and specified by the Peace Treaties, for a war indemnity, presupposes that the damages inflicted by the war are considered to be illegally caused. This is the meaning of Article 231 of the Peace Treaty of Versailles establishing Germany's war guilt:

> The Allied and Associated Governments affirm and Germany accepts the responsibility of Germany and her allies for causing all the loss and damage to which the Allied and Associated Governments and their nationals have been subjected as a consequence of the war imposed upon them by the aggression of Germany and her allies.

The statement that the war was "imposed" upon the Allied and Associated Governments "by the aggression of Germany and her Allies" means that Germany and her Allies violated international law by resorting to the war. Otherwise the obligation to repair the damage caused by the war would not be justifiable, since the damage would not have been illegally caused. Only on the basis of the *bellum justum* doctrine is "war guilt" possible.

When the Second World War broke out, the legal situation was different from that at the outbreak of the First World War. The Axis Powers were contracting parties to the Briand-Kellogg Pact by which resorting to a war of aggression is made a delict; and Germany, by attacking Poland and Russia, violated, in addition to the Briand-Kellogg Pact, non-aggression pacts with the attacked States. Any inquiry into the authorship of the second World War does not raise problems of extraordinary complexity. Neither the *questio juris* nor the *questio facti* offers any serious difficulty to a tribunal. Hence, there is no reason to renounce a criminal charge made against the persons morally responsible for the outbreak of World War II. Insofar as this is also a question of the constitutional law of the Axis Powers, the answer is simplified by the fact that these States were under more or less dictatorial regimes, so that the number of persons who had the legal power of leading their country into war is in each of the Axis States very small. In Germany it is probably the Fuehrer alone; in Italy, the Duce and the King; and in Japan, the Prime Minister and the Emperor. If the assertion attributed to Louis XIV "l'Etat c'est moi" is applicable to any dictatorship, the punishment of the dictator amounts almost to a punishment of the State. Another question is whether it will be actually possible to lay hold on these persons in order to bring them to justice before a national or international tribunal.

16. The punishment of war crimes

PUBLIC OPINION DEMANDS not only making responsible the authors of the war but also, in particular, bringing to justice the so-called war criminals, that is to say, the persons who have violated the rules of warfare. This demand plays an important role in the Declaration of Moscow.* War crimes in the specific sense of the term are acts by which rules of international law regulating the conduct of war are violated. They are committed by members of the armed forces of the belligerents. The term "war crimes" sometimes comprises also all hostilities in arms committed by individuals who are not members of the armed forces, acts of illegitimate warfare committed by private individuals who take up arms against the enemy, and, further, espionage, war treason, and all marauding acts. Most of the acts constituting violations of the rules of warfare are at the same time violations of general criminal law, such as murder, pillage, theft, incendiarism, rape, and the like. "The principle," says Garner, "that the individual soldier who commits acts in violation of the laws of war when these acts are at the same time offenses against the general criminal law should be liable to

* Since the United States, Great Britain, and Soviet Russia made the punishment of war criminals one of their war aims, it is fruitless to raise the question whether it is advisable, from the point of view of the future peace, to institute after the conclusion of the war or even during the war legal procedures for the punishment of war crimes. In a discussion on the establishment of an international criminal court which took place at the Thirty-third Conference of the International Law Association held at Stockholm in 1924, Sir Graham Bower said:

"There is no nation in the world which has not violated the laws of war, and there is no army or navy in the world which has not committed war crimes." And further: "What will be the consequence [of a punishment of war criminals]? When the soldiers and sailors have finished fighting, when they are ready to shake hands over a treaty of peace, then the lawyers are to begin a war of accusation and counter-accusation and re-crimination, which will be worse than war. General Sherman said, 'War is hell,' and he spoke the truth; but with all due respect, I submit that if this proposal were adopted, it would make peace a hell." Sir Graham Bower terminated his speech by saying: "A bas la guerre des procès, vive la paix de l'oubli et de l'espérance."—*The International Law Association, Report of the Thirty-third Conference* (held at Stockholm, September 8 to 13, 1924), (London, 1925), pp. 93, 95. Cf. also: C. Arnold Anderson, "The Utility of the Proposed Trial and Punishment of Enemy Leaders," *The American Political Science Review* (1943), Vol. 37, pp. 1081 ff.

trial and punishment by the courts of the injured adversary in case he falls into the hands of the authorities thereof, has long been maintained...." * The acts in question are considered to be punishable by the courts of the injured State because they constitute crimes according to its national law. But almost all acts of war, including acts of legitimate warfare, constitute crimes according to criminal law, since acts of war are acts of forcible deprivation of life, liberty, property, forbidden by criminal law. Nevertheless, acts of legitimate warfare are not punishable by the courts of the State whose subjects are the victims. A State which punishes for murder or incendiarism soldiers who, as members of the armed forces of the enemy, have killed in battle soldiers of the armed forces of the State claiming jurisdiction, or have burned houses of the latter's citizens, openly violates international law. What deprives these acts of their criminal character? What excludes the criminal responsibility of the individuals who have performed these acts? The usual answer is that these acts are in conformity with international law which permits the belligerents to deprive forcibly the members of the armed forces of the enemy of their lives and freedom, to destroy property of their citizens, and the like. They are "legitimate" acts of war only when they are performed in conformity with international law; "... otherwise they are murder or theft as the case may be and their authors are liable to punishment as criminals." † The tenor of this doctrine may be formulated as follows: the fact that an act forbidden as a crime by national law is "in conformity with"—i.e., permitted by—international law, deprives the

* J. W. Garner, *International Law and the World War* (1920), Vol. II, p. 472.
† *Ibid.*, p. 473, following Renault, "De l'application du droit pénal aux faits de guerre," *Revue Générale de Droit International Public* (1918), Vol. 25, p. 10.

act of its criminal character; if the act is forbidden by international law, too, it retains its criminal character.

This doctrine is untenable. The statement that acts of legitimate warfare are "permitted" by international law means that international law does not "forbid" them. To be legally "permitted" means to be legally not forbidden. An act is legally forbidden if it is the condition of a sanction. The statement that international law does not forbid a certain act means that international law does not attach any sanction to it. The negative fact that international law does not forbid certain acts because it does not attach sanctions to them cannot exclude the legal possibility of national law attaching sanctions to those acts and thus forbidding them. National law attaches sanctions to many acts which are not forbidden—and that means "permitted" (in the negative sense of the term) —by international law, without violating international law. An individual, citizen of State A, when committing theft against an individual, citizen of State B, in the territory of State A, does not violate international law. The latter does not forbid such an act and does not make State A responsible for it. But State B does not violate international law by punishing the thief when he falls into the hands of its authorities. In fact, that an act treated as criminal by national law is not forbidden (and hence "permitted" in a negative sense) by international law does not deprive the act of its criminal character.

However, the term "permission" may have a positive sense. It may mean "authorization." The law "authorizes" an individual by conferring upon the individual a legal power, a "right" in the technical sense of the term. The law "authorizes" an individual to perform an act to which the law attaches a legal effect, the legal effect intended by the acting individual. Killing, wounding, capturing of human beings in war, unlike legal transactions or actions brought before a court, are not acts by which legal effects are intended. They are "permitted" by international law only in the negative sense of the term. This is especially true if war, as many writers assume, is not a legal action authorized by international law as reaction to an international "delict," that is, as "just war," and otherwise forbidden as a delict. It is squarely on the basis of the *bellum justum* theory that the fallacy can be proved of the doctrine that an act which is permitted by international law must not be punished according to national law; and that, as a logical consequence, an act which is forbidden by international law may be punished according to national law. Normal acts of warfare performed by members of armed forces involved in an unjust war forbidden by general international law or by a particular treaty, such as the Briand-Kellogg Pact, cannot be considered to be "permitted," either in a negative or in a positive sense, since the war as such is forbidden and, consequently, all the single acts which in their totality constitute the war must be considered as forbidden.* Nevertheless, a State which punishes a member of the armed forces of the enemy guilty of an unjust war for having killed in battle a member of the armed forces of the State claiming jurisdiction violates international law. The fact that the act is forbidden by international law does not maintain the criminal character which it may have according to national law.

That a State violates international law if it punishes, ac-

* The distinction between acts of "legitimate" and acts of "illegitimate" warfare performed in a war forbidden by general or particular international law is possible only insofar as an act of "legitimate" warfare constitutes only the violation of the rule forbidding war, whereas an act of "illegitimate" warfare constitutes a violation not only of that rule but also of a rule concerning warfare. It is quite possible that by one and the same act two different legal rules are violated, and that two different rules attach to one and the same act two different sanctions.

cording to its national law, a member of the armed forces of the enemy for an act of legitimate warfare, can be explained only by the fact that by so doing one State makes an individual responsible for the act of another State. According to international law, the act in question must be imputed to the enemy State and not to the individual who in the service of his State has performed the act. It cannot be considered as a crime of the individual because it must not be considered as his personal act at all. General international law, as a rule, forbids a State to make a person individually responsible for an act committed as an act of another State. Consequently, the individual performing an act of war as an act of his State must not be punished for this act by the enemy State, even if the act constitutes a violation of international law, even if the war as such is forbidden or the act in itself constitutes a so-called war crime. For an act performed by an individual at the command or with the authorization of his government is an act of State, even if it constitutes a violation of international law; and responsibility for such a violation of international law rests, according to general international law, upon the State collectively, not upon the individual who in the service of his State has performed the act.* Otherwise no violation of international law in general and the rules regarding warfare in particular *by States* would be possible. "Violations of rules regarding warfare," writes Oppenheim, "are war crimes only when committed without an order of the bel-

---

* Hugh H. L. Bellot, "A Permanent International Criminal Court," *The International Law Association, Report of the Thirty-first Conference* (1923), Vol. I, p. 73. "An order by the ... Government cannot make that lawful which is unlawful by International Law." That is true, but the fact that an act is "unlawful by International Law" does not necessarily constitute the individual responsibility of the perpetrator. As a rule, it constitutes only the collective responsibility of the State whose government issued the command.

ligerent government concerned. If members of the armed
forces commit violations *by order* of their government"—
and that means if the violation of the rules of warfare has the
character of an act of State—"they are not war criminals,
and may not be punished by the enemy; the latter may, however, resort to reprisals." * The responsibility of the State
realized by reprisals is collective, not individual responsibility. If the war crime is an act of State, the collective
responsibility of the State for this act, as a rule, excludes individual responsibility for it. † The fact that the act is forbidden by international law does not maintain the criminal
character which it may have according to national law. If an
act is forbidden by international law as a war crime the perpetrator personally may be punished by the injured State
according to its national law if he falls into the hands of its
authorities as prisoner of war only in case it is recognized
that the act is not an act of the enemy State. ‡

This is the consequence of the generally recognized principle that no State has jurisdiction over the acts of another
State. Suspension of this principle must not be considered
as one of the effects of the outbreak of war upon the relations between the belligerents. § The rules of general customary international law remain, in principle, in force in

* L. Oppenheim, *International Law* (1st to 5th eds.), Vol. II, § 253.
† A von Verdross, *Voelkerrecht* (1937), p. 298, correctly formulates
the rule concerned as follows: "Punishment [of a prisoner of war for a war
crime] is inadmissible if the act has not been performed [of the accused
person's] own account but can be imputed to his home State." An act
which is to be imputed to the State is an act of State.
‡ Cf. George Manner, "The Legal Nature and Punishment of Criminal
Acts of Violence Contrary to the Laws of War," *American Journal of International Law* (1943), Vol. 37, pp. 407 ff., 433.
§ A. Mérignhac, "De la sanction des infractions au droit des gens,"
Revue Générale de droit international public (1917), Vol. 24, p. 49, asserts:
"La théorie de l'acte de gouvernement est une théorie de paix, qui disparaît
au cours des hostilités." This assertion is without foundation in positive
international law.

time of war. The rule according to which the collective responsibility of the State for its acts excludes the individual responsibility of the perpetrator is by its very nature destined to play an important role not only in time of peace but also in time of war. War itself is one of the most characteristic acts of State; the principle in question is a necessary protection of individuals who by national law are obliged or authorized as organs of their State to perform acts considered to be necessary in the interest of the State.

However, the rule of general customary international law granting acts of State immunity from the jurisdiction of another State has some exceptions, as has been pointed out. Does the rule that prisoners of war be subjected to the law and jurisdiction of the captor State constitute, with respect to violations of the rules of warfare, a restriction on the principle of the immunity of the State from the jurisdiction of another State? Without examining that part of the question involving the principle of a State's immunity from the jurisdiction of another State, some writers have maintained that the fact that a war crime is committed as an act of State does not deprive the act of its character as crime punishable by the injured State according to its national law.* This view, however, is more than questionable. Criminal jurisdiction of the captor State over war prisoners constitutes a restriction of the rule according to which the members of the armed forces of a foreign State are exempt from the jurisdiction of the State on the territory of which they are staying. Since jurisdiction over prisoners of war is based on a restric-

---

* This view is adopted also in the 6th edition of Oppenheim, *op. cit.* (1940). Vol. II, § 253, edited by H. Lauterpacht. Here it is said of the opinion advocated in all the five foregoing editions: "It is difficult to regard it as expressing a sound legal principle." In the sixth edition the fact that a war crime is an act of State is not clearly distinguished from the fact that it is performed at superior command. See *infra,* p. 104.

tion of another rule, a restrictive interpretation of the rule conferring jurisdiction over prisoners of war upon the captor State is well founded. There is no reason to interpret the rule concerned as a restriction of still another rule, namely, the rule that no State has jurisdiction over the acts of another State, and to allow the captor State to punish a prisoner of war for acts committed as acts of his State without the latter's consent. Jurisdiction of the State over individuals who, as prisoners of war, are staying on its own territory can also be based on the general principle that any State has exclusive jurisdiction over all persons and things within its territory. Among the restrictions to this principle, the rule regarding the immunity of a foreign State stands certainly in the first place. A State cannot elude this rule of general international law by declaring the act of a foreign State a crime in the sense of its (the former's) national law and prosecute the individual perpetrator of the act if he falls into the hands of its authorities. Prosecution of an individual for an act that has been performed as an act of a foreign State is directed against the foreign State itself.

A clear exception is established by the rules regarding espionage and war treason. General international law authorizes the State against which acts of espionage or war treason have been committed to punish the perpetrators as criminals, even if the acts concerned have been committed at the command or with the authorization of the enemy government. In contradistinction to other war crimes, the States in whose interest espionage or war treason is committed are not obliged to prevent and to punish acts of this nature. The State which employs spies or makes use of war treason in its own interest does not violate international law * and is not responsible for these acts.

* Oppenheim, *op. cit.*, Vol. II. pp. 328 ff.

The individual, however, who commits these acts, may, according to international law, be punished by the injured State. In these cases, general international law establishes only the individual responsibility of the perpetrators.

Insofar as individual responsibility for violation of the rules of warfare committed as acts of State is, according to general international law, excluded, punishment for such acts by a national court of the enemy or by an international court without violation of international law is possible only with the consent of the home State of the delinquent—that is to say, on the basis of an international treaty concluded with the State for whose acts the individual perpetrators are to be punished. Only by such treaty can jurisdiction over the individuals concerned be conferred upon a national court of the enemy or an international court. The norm of conventional international law establishing their individual responsibility may have retroactive force.

An international treaty as the legal basis of trials of war criminals is also necessary if prisoners of war are to be tried after the conclusion of peace for violation of the rules of warfare not committed as acts of State. For, according to general international law as well as the Geneva Convention of 1929, all prisoners of war must be released after the conclusion of peace. Any restriction of this rule is possible only with the consent of the home State of the prisoner. It stands to reason that the home State of the war criminal has jurisdiction over him, too. The jurisdiction of the captor State over war prisoners for war crimes not committed as acts of State is only a concurrent one. Whereas the captor State is authorized by international law to punish members of the armed forces of the enemy for war crimes, the home State is obliged to punish its own war criminals; and the injured State has a right to demand the punishment.

Article 3 of the 1907 Hague Convention respecting the Laws and Customs of War on Land states:

> A belligerent party which violates the provisions of the said Regulations [annexed to the Convention] shall, if the case demands, be liable to pay compensation. It shall be responsible for all acts committed by persons forming part of its armed forces.

That means that a belligerent State is responsible for violations of the rules of warfare committed by members of its armed forces, whether these acts have or have not the character of acts of State. The responsibility for war crimes which have not the character of acts of State implies the duty to punish the criminals.

17. War crimes as violations of international or national law

MOST OF THE WRITERS on international law maintain that war crimes constitute only penal offenses against national law, and that they have only "municipal" character, since international law does not provide punishment of the offenders.* This is not correct. If the violations of the international rules of warfare are acts of State, they have, according to present positive law, no "penal" character in that the perpetrators are not punishable according to national criminal law; but they are international delicts for which the State is responsible, i.e., liable to sanctions which may be interpreted as "punishment." † If the violations of the rules of warfare are not acts of State, and if they are at the same time crimes according to national law, they

* Cf. Manner, *op. cit.*, p. 407.
† Cf. *supra*, p. 73.

have a double character; they are penal offenses against international and at the same time against national law. General international law, it is true, does not directly determine the penalty to be inflicted upon the criminal. But international law obliges the States whose subjects have, as members of their own armed forces, violated the laws of warfare, to punish the criminals; and general international law authorizes the belligerents to punish an enemy subject who has fallen into the hands of their authorities as prisoner of war for having violated, prior to his capture, the laws of warfare. It is with respect to this authorization to punish enemy war criminals, that war crimes are usually defined as "such hostile or other acts of soldiers or other individuals as may be punished by the enemy on capture of the offenders." * This definition is not quite correct since it refers only to war crimes in their relation to the enemy and ignores the fact that war crimes are delicts also in relationship to the State whose subjects have committed the crimes, that these crimes are directly determined by international law, and that the home State of the delinquents is obliged by international law (not only authorized as is the enemy) to punish the criminals. By obliging States to punish their own war criminals and by authorizing States to punish enemy war criminals, international law provides, at least indirectly, for punishment of war criminals. It leaves to national law to specify the penalty; even the death penalty is not excluded by international law. Consequently, it is incorrect to speak of "absence of international war crimes." The obligation of the States to punish their own war criminals is but a consequence of their general obligation to execute international law within the sphere of validity of their own legal orders. Such an obligation is expressly stipulated,

* Oppenheim, op. cit., Vol. II, p. 451.

for instance, by Article I of the Hague Land Warfare Conventions of 1899 and 1907, by Article 8 of the Red Cross Convention of 1906, by Article 29 of the Red Cross Convention of 1929, and by Article 21 of the Hague Convention of 1907 concerning Adaptation of the Principles of the Geneva Convention to Maritime Warfare. The national criminal laws which attach penalties to war crimes, i.e., to acts forbidden by the international law of warfare, are enacted in fulfillment of the State's obligation to enforce the international law within the State's sphere of power. The application of national law to the war criminal is at the same time execution of international law. The national law is an intermediate stage made necessary by the State constitution authorizing the courts to apply only norms created by the law-making organs of the State. If no such constitutional restriction exists, or if, according to the constitution, international law is considered part of the national law, a direct application of the international rules of warfare by the courts of the State is possible. Since, however, these rules do not specify the punishment, an act of national law determining the penalties for war crimes is always necessary if these war crimes do not constitute at the same time ordinary crimes according to the criminal law of the State.

If the crimes in question constituted merely offenses of national law, if their punishment were not application of international law, then it would hardly be possible to speak of war crimes. They are war crimes only insofar as they constitute violations of the rules of warfare, and these rules are, in the first place, norms of international law. National criminal law attaches penalties to ordinary crimes, such as murder, theft, and the like. If a code of military criminal law attaches penalties to the killing of the wounded, refusal of quarter, making use of poisoned arms, pillage by members of the armed forces, and the like, it does so in order to enforce the norms of international law forbidding these acts. In the absence of such a code of national law and of the possibility of direct application of international law, so-called war criminals could be punished only for having committed ordinary crimes. The misuse of the Red Cross flag would never be made a crime by national criminal law if the latter had not the purpose of executing the Geneva Convention.

18. The plea of superior command

NATIONAL COURTS WHICH, on the basis of national law, try individuals for war crimes are confronted with a serious difficulty when the act which constitutes the war crime has been committed at superior command. This does not necessarily imply that the act is an act of State. It is an act of State only if the command itself is an act of State, and that is the case only if the command was issued by the government (Head of State, cabinet, member of cabinet, parliament), or issued at the command or with the authorization of the government. The fact that an act is an act of State constitutes, in the first place, a problem of general international law * which, as a rule, excludes individual responsibility for an act of State. The fact that an act is performed at a superior command constitutes a problem of national criminal law. It is the problem whether the plea of superior command is to be admitted by national criminal law as a defense against prosecution of an individual charged with a war crime, whether the perpetrator who executed the command, or only the individual who issued the command, can be made responsible and be punished for the act.

---

* Responsibility for acts of State is, of course, not only a problem of international but also of national law. See *supra*, p. 82.

As to the admissibility of the plea of superior command, the different positive legal orders as well as the opinions of jurists differ. From a military point of view, the plea must certainly be admitted. Discipline is possible only on the basis of unconditional obedience of the subordinate to the superior, and the obedience of the subordinate has its necessary complement in the exclusive responsibility of the superior. Article 347 of the Basic Field Manual: Rules of Land Warfare (FM 27-10), published by the War Department of the United States in 1940 (after enumerating the possible offenses by armed forces) stipulates:

> Individuals of the armed forces will not be punished for these offenses in case they are committed under the orders or sanction of their government or commanders. The commanders ordering the commission of such acts, or under whose authority they are committed by their troops, may be punished by the belligerent into whose hands they may fall.

Some national legal orders do not admit the plea of superior command if the command itself is illegal and as such void *ab initio*. The execution of a legal command can never be punished as a crime. If the command is issued as a general or individual norm by the government or by a subordinate organ authorized by the government's order, the command is rarely illegal in the sense of being void *ab initio*. The general or individual norm issued by the government is normally not void *ab initio,* though it may be voidable, even if it is not in conformity with a superior norm of national law. This is the case if the war crime has been committed under the sanction of an "unconstitutional" statute or an "illegal" decree of the government, or an "illegal" army regulation. As long as such a norm is not invalidated by the competent authority, it is valid; and as long as it is valid it has to be considered in relation to the individual who executes it as a legal command. Cases of absolute nullity (not mere annullability) of acts of Government are very rare. Moreover, the legal power conferred by national law and, in particular, by the law of autocratic States like Nazi Germany, upon the government—and that means, upon the Head of the State as commander-in-chief of the armed forces with respect to the conduct of war—is almost unlimited. The government is nearly always in a position to justify its acts from the point of view of national law by the necessities of war. Consequently, it is difficult to repudiate the plea of superior command by the argument that the command was "illegal," in case the command has been issued by the government or is based on a command of the government. The argument of illegality of the command as justification for repudiating the plea of superior command is practically restricted to cases of commands issued by relatively subordinate organs without authorization on the part of their government.

According to the law of some States, the plea of superior command can be rejected only if the command was manifestly and indisputably contrary to law. It is not sufficient that the command was objectively illegal. The command must be "universally known to everybody, including also the accused, to be without any doubt whatever against the law." * Such cases are very rare. If the illegality of the command consists in a violation of international law, it is almost impossible to suppose that the command is "universally known" to be "without any doubt" against the law. In this

* Decision of the German Reichsgericht in Leipzig in the case of the *Llandovery Castle,* quoted by Claud Mullins, *The Leipzig Trials* (1921), p. 131.

case the situation is totally different from that where the illegality of the command constitutes a violation of general criminal law. Everybody knows, or is in a position to know, what the general criminal law of his country forbids. But can it reasonably be assumed that every soldier knows what international law forbids? What otherwise would be a violation of international law is, according to the same international law, permitted as reprisal. This is of particular importance with respect to the rules of warfare, since the only sanctions provided by international law against a violation of these rules are reprisals. How can a soldier know that a command that violates the rules of warfare is not a reprisal and therefore permitted? How can he consider such a command to be "without any doubt whatever" against the law? The idea of justice which is the basis of national criminal law and in particular the basis of military criminal law, is certainly not favorable to the prosecution of individuals who commit war crimes in response to a superior command. Since most of the war crimes the punishment of which is demanded, and in particular many of the politically important war crimes, are committed at superior commands that can hardly be supposed to be manifestly and indisputably illegal, national courts applying national criminal law are certainly not fitted for the punishment of war criminals if the plea of superior command shall not be admitted. Under this condition the national courts of the accused are especially ill-fitted. Those courts are still more inclined to admit the plea of superior command than are the courts of the enemy. This has been proved by the famous trials of German war criminals after the first World War.*

* Cf. Mullins, *op. cit., passim.*

19. The jurisdiction over prisoners of war

ACCORDING TO a generally accepted view, mentioned above, a belligerent has jurisdiction over prisoners of war for war crimes committed before capture. National military courts exercising jurisdiction over prisoners of war are confronted with the difficulty that it is, at least, doubtful whether military tribunals can prosecute enemy war criminals after the conclusion of peace. As pointed out, if international law is not to be violated, prisoners of war must be released at the end of the war, even if they have been sentenced for committing war crimes and even if their terms of imprisonment have not yet expired.* In any case, prisoners of war charged with war crimes but not yet tried and sentenced must be released. In order to overcome this difficulty, it has been suggested "that the armistice agreement shall contain provisions for the surrender of the war criminals of the enemy in order to give the victorious Powers the opportunity to try the criminals through their national courts before the conclusion of peace." † But it is doubtful whether individuals surrendered by one belligerent to the other on the basis of an international treaty—the armistice agreement—are really "prisoners of war." Prisoners of war are, according to the definition given in Article 1, Section 2, of the Convention relating to the treatment of prisoners of war, signed at Geneva, July 27, 1929, for prisoners captured in sea and air warfare,

* W. E. Hall, *A Treatise on International Law* (1924), Sec. 135. Oppenheim, *op. cit.*, Vol. II, p. 459, maintains that a belligerent has the right to carry out the punishment inflicted on a war criminal even beyond the duration of the war.

† Suggestion of the Lord Chancellor in the House of Lords, October, 1942, mentioned by Manner, *op. cit.*, p. 433.

... persons belonging to the armed forces of belligerents
who are captured by the enemy in the course of operations
of maritime or aerial war. . . .

Persons extradited by one of the belligerents to the other
in execution of a treaty of armistice can hardly be considered as captured in the course of military operations. The
legal basis of the jurisdiction claimed over such persons by
the enemy is not the rule of international law concerning
jurisdiction over prisoners of war, but the international
treaty by which the State whose subjects are sought for
trial consents to their trial by the enemy. By the provisions
of the armistice agreement, jurisdiction over the persons
in question may be conferred upon the enemy. Since such
persons are not war prisoners, in the strict sense of the term,
the courts of the enemy are not compelled to terminate the
trial before the conclusion of peace. The accused persons
are in the same legal position as individuals extradited in
conformity with a treaty of extradition in time of peace.
From a legal point of view, there is no essential difference
between such an armistice agreement and a peace treaty
embodying the same terms. By such a treaty, the legal ob-
stacles which impede post-war jurisdiction of the enemy
over war criminals can be removed. And by such a treaty
jurisdiction can be extended over war crimes having the
character of acts of State and individuals can be made responsible for acts of State.

This seems to be the true function of Article 228 of the
Peace Treaty of Versailles, which runs as follows:

> The German Government recognizes the right of the Al-
> lied and Associated Powers to bring before military tribu-
> nals persons accused of having committed acts in violation
> of the laws and customs of war. Such persons shall, if found
> guilty, be sentenced to punishments laid down by law.

By choosing the term "recognize," the authors of the Peace
Treaty seem to have attributed to Article 228 a declaratory
character only. But without the consent of the German Government given in Article 228, the military tribunals of the
Allied and Associated Powers had no right to try persons for
war crimes after the conclusion of peace. Article 228 does
not expressly include war crimes which have the character
of acts of State. But the fact that it does not exclude them,
and that, according to its wording, the German Government agrees to the prosecution by enemy military tribunals
of their nationals for all acts committed in violation of the
laws and customs of war, Article 228 may be interpreted as
the necessary consent of the German Government to the
punishment of Germans for having committed war crimes
having the character of acts of State, as the establishment of
the individual responsibility of the persons concerned. To
avoid any doubt at the close of the second World War, it
would be advisable to insert into any future international
treaties conferring upon national or international courts
jurisdiction over war criminals an express provision including war crimes which have the character of acts of State.*

20. International criminal jurisdiction

AS TO THE QUESTION what kind of tribunal shall be authorized to try war criminals, national or international, there

---

* In case the territory of one belligerent is occupied by the armed forces
of the other belligerent, the occupant seems to be in a position to establish a special tribunal to try subjects of the enemy, even members of its
government, arrested after the armistice by the authorities of the occupant on the occupied territory (hence not considered to be prisoners of
war) for having committed war crimes. This is the assumption upon which
Max Radin's *The Day of Reckoning* (1943) is based. It is, however,
doubtful whether the rules of general international law regulating the
rights and duties of the occupant are favorable to such a procedure.

can be little doubt that an international court is much more
fitted for this task than a national civil or military court.*
Only a court established by an international treaty, to which
not only the victorious but also the vanquished States are
contracting parties, will not meet with certain difficulties
with which a national court would be confronted. For a
.treaty by which jurisdiction over war criminals is conferred
upon an international court may establish individual responsibility for war crimes that have the character of acts
of State. It may also exclude the plea of superior command
if this should seem necessary to the development of international justice. Now only an international court—international not only with respect to its legal basis but also with
respect to its composition—can be above any suspicion of
partiality. National courts, and in particular national military courts, inevitably are open to suspicion. Trials of war
prisoners conducted by military courts during war may in-
duce the enemy to take retaliatory measures of the same

* C. C. Hyde, "Punishment of War Criminals," *Proceedings of the American Society of International Law at Its Thirty-Seventh Annual Meeting
Held at Washington, D. C.* (1943), p. 43, says: "It is conceivable that the
Allied Powers may prefer to remain severally free to try and punish such
alien enemy actors as are surrendered to them by domestic tribunals empowered to pass judgment on the conduct of those individuals and to
apply penalties. At first glance this would appear to be a simple and
unobjectionable procedure, and one free from certain difficulties to be
encountered in any other. If, however, recourse to this method were
productive of wholesale convictions and the application of innumerable
penalties, the prosecuting victors might have difficulty in convincing
society at large that the courts employed for the purpose were other than
political tools; and the persons subjected to punishment might be regarded
abroad as well as at home as martyrs.... A court or courts composed
solely of neutral nationals would more easily command respect for decisions
adverse to the claims and defenses of accused persons, and unless unduly
fettered by the terms of the relevant treaty, might prove to be highly
useful as expositors of international law. Moreover, the willingness of the
Allied Powers to test and establish their grievances before neutral judges
would inspire a widespread and decent respect for their stand."

kind, although reprisals against prisoners of war are forbidden by the Geneva Convention. Such misuse of the law
can be avoided by transferring the punishment of war criminals to an international tribunal which commences its activity after the conclusion of peace and consequently is in
a position to fulfill its task in an atmosphere not poisoned
by the passions of war. Internationalization of the legal·
procedure against war criminals would have the great advantage of making the punishment, to a certain extent, uni-
form. If war criminals are subjected to various national
courts, as provided by Article 229 of the Treaty of Versailles, it is very likely that these courts will "result in conflicting decisions and varying penalties." *

* Bellot, *op. cit.*, p. 421. Art. 21 of the *Statute of the International Penal
Court*, adopted by the 34th Conference of the International Law Association of 1926 (*Report of the Thirty-fourth Conference*, p. 118) runs as
follows:

> The jurisdiction of the Court shall extend to all charges of
> (a) Violations of international obligations of a penal character com-
> mitted by the subjects or citizens of one State or by a heimatlos
> against another State or its subjects or citizens, (b) Violations of any
> treaty, convention or declaration binding on the States parties to the
> convention of (place) dated........day of........, which regulate the
> methods and conduct of warfare, (c) Violations of the laws and cus-
> toms of war generally accepted as binding by civilized nations.—
> Without prejudice to the original jurisdiction of the Court as herein-
> before defined, the Court shall have power to deal with cases of a
> penal character referred to it by the Council or Assembly of the ·
> League of Nations for trial, or for inquiry and report.—In the event of
> a dispute as to whether the Court has jurisdiction 'the matter shall
> be settled by the decision of the Court.

In the "Report of the Permanent International Criminal Court Committee," *ibid.*, p. 110, it is said: "The body of opinion supporting the
creation of an International Criminal Court is very considerable. In a
paper read to the Grotius Society in March, 1916, and published in the
September number of the *Nineteenth Century*, Dr. Bellot suggested the
establishment of such a Court. It was recommended by the British Committee of Enquiry into Breaches of the Laws of War, and such recommendation was endorsed by the International Commission on War Crimes
appointed by the Versailles Conference by a majority of eight to one. This

It is the jurisdiction of the victorious States over the war criminals of the enemy which the Three Power Declaration signed in Moscow demands. The persons who have committed war crimes shall ". . . be brought back to the scene of their crimes and judged on the spot by the peoples whom they have outraged." War crimes which "have no particular geographical localization" shall be punished by ". . . joint decision of the Governments of the Allies." It is quite understandable that during a war peoples who are victims of war crimes wish to take the law in their own hands and punish those whom they judge to be criminals. But after a war is over, minds that have been closed open again to the consideration that criminal jurisdiction exercised by injured States over enemy subjects may be regarded as vengeance rather than justice and is consequently not the best means to guarantee future peace. This is particularly true with respect to crimes which are acts of the enemy State.

---

recommendation was, however, rejected by the Supreme Council. It was subsequently recommended by the Committee of Hague Jurists, which drafted the Statute for the Permanent Court of International Justice. It was advocated by Lord Phillimore and Dr. Bellot in papers read at the Buenos Aires Conference of the International Law Association in 1922. Both authors of these papers suggested that the jurisdiction of the Court should extend to non-military as well as military offenses. But the conference limited it to the latter, and it was resolved 'That in the opinion of this Conference the creation of an International Criminal Court is essential in the interest of justice and that the Conference is of the opinion that the matter is one of urgency.' " In 1926 the International Penal Law Association at its Conference held in Brussels suggested the conferring of criminal jurisdiction upon the Permanent Court of International Justice. At the International Conference on the Repression of Terrorism, held at the initiative of the Council of the League of Nations, at Geneva on November 1 to 16, 1937, a Convention for the Creation of an International Criminal Court for the trial of persons accused of acts of terrorism was signed. See *Proceedings of the International Conference on the Repression of Terrorism*, Series of League of Nations Publications, Legal, 1938, V. 3. Cf., also M. O. Hudson, "The Proposed International Criminal Court," *American Journal of International Law* (1938), Vol. 32, pp. 549 ff.

Even if the principle that no State has jurisdiction over acts of another State were considered as not applicable in time of war—which is, at least, very doubtful *—it is from a political point of view most advisable to try persons accused of such acts through an international court with the consent of their own State. To get this consent in the armistice or peace treaty concluded with the vanquished State is not too difficult. For the new government established after the defeat has sufficient reasons to disavow, in its own interest, the internationally illegal acts of its predecessor.

The punishment of war criminals should be an act of international justice, not the satisfaction of a thirst for revenge. It is not compatible with the idea of international justice that only the vanquished States should be obliged to surrender their subjects to the jurisdiction of an international tribunal for the punishment of war crimes. The victorious States, too, should be willing to transfer jurisdiction over their own subjects who have offended the laws of warfare to the same independent and impartial international tribunal. † Only if the victors submit themselves to the same

---

* Cf. *supra*, pp. 97 ff.

† Hyde, *op. cit.*, p. 43, says: "Should the work of any tribunals be confined objectively to the trial and possible conviction of members of the Axis forces, or should it embrace members of the Allied forces charged by their enemies with committing offenses against the laws of war? The matter needs careful thought. Confidence in the high purpose of the Allied Powers would doubtless be enhanced in every quarter if the courts to be employed were given a comprehensive jurisdiction to pass upon the conduct of any person of any nationality, regardless of the belligerent on whose side he served. If, however, a member of an Allied force were found guilty, as charged, the matter of inflicting a penalty would call for definite arrangement. An Allied Power might be expected to decline to agree to surrender a convicted member of its forces to an Axis Power for punishment under its auspices. Doubtless an Allied Power would insist on a scheme for the punishment of members of its own services by its own agencies within its own domain, if they were to be subjected to prosecution."

law which they wish to impose upon the vanquished States will the idea of international justice be preserved. As far as penalties are concerned, the treaty establishing the jurisdiction of the court should authorize the latter to inflict upon the guilty person the penalty provided by the criminal law of his own State. If the court has jurisdiction over persons who, in their capacity as organs of a State, have violated international law by resorting to or provoking war, the treaty establishing the court may determine the penalties or authorize the court to fix them according to its discretion.

The punishment of war crimes by an international tribunal, and particularly the punishment of crimes which have the character of acts of State, would certainly meet with much less resistance, since it would hurt national feelings much less, if it were carried out within the framework of a general reform of international law. The aim of this reform should be to complete the collective responsibility of States for violations of international law by the individual responsibility of the persons who, as agents of the State, have committed the acts by which international law has been violated.* Such a reform can be carried out success-

* The Conference of the International Penal Law Association held at Brussels, 1926, passed unanimously the following resolutions: "1. That criminal jurisdiction be granted to the Permanent Court of International Justice. 2. That it be consulted, regarding the settlement of conflicts of jurisdiction, judicial or legislative, which may arise between different States.... 3. That the Criminal Permanent Court shall hear all cases for penal responsibilities brought against States consequent upon an unjust aggression and for violations of International Law. It shall impose penal sanctions and measures for security upon the offending State. 4. That the Permanent Court shall hear cases of individual responsibilities which may arise from the crime of aggression as well as crimes and accessory crimes or misdemeanors and all violations of international law committed in time of peace or in time of war and particularly Common Law offences which by reason of the nationality of the victim of the presumed offenders can be considered in this or by other States as being international offences and as

fully only on the basis of a treaty constituting a League of States whose main organ is a court endowed with compulsory jurisdiction, such as proposed in the first part of the present study. Criminal jurisdiction could be conferred upon the court competent to decide the disputes between the members of the League or upon a special chamber of the court. If the court has competence in criminal matters some of the judges must be experts in criminal law.*

If individual responsibility in all the international relations of States is to be established by providing for punishment of guilty persons, the question arises as to the conditions under which an act which constitutes a violation of international law has the character of a punishable crime in the strict sense of the term. Not every act which constitutes a violation of law is a punishable crime. Which violations of international law committed by a State are of such a nature that it is justifiable to punish the individuals who in their capacity as organs of the State have performed the acts which constitute the violation of law? There is no difficulty in answering this question if, as in the case of a war crime, the act is a violation of international law and at the same time a violation of national criminal law. If, however, the act is not a "crime" according to national criminal law, its punishment provided by an international treaty is justifiable only if it is by its very nature a "crime." But what is a

---

constituting a menace to the peace of the world. 5. That the Permanent Court shall have the jurisdiction over individuals who may have committed crimes or offenses which cannot be submitted to the jurisdiction of a particular State, owing to the fact that the territory on which such offenses have been committed is unknown or where the sovereignty is disputed."—
Revue Internationale de Droit Pénal (1926), Vol. 3, p. 466.

* In Annex II a draft of treaty stipulations is presented to be inserted into the draft of a Covenant for the P.L.M.P. (Annex I) in case individual responsibility for violations of international law (international criminal jurisdiction) is to be established.

"crime" in contradistinction to other violations of law, and what is the criterion of a crime—not *de lege lata* but *de lege ferenda*—which justifies the specific sanction characterized as "punishment"? The usual answer to this question is that an act is a punishable crime if, according to the opinion of the law-maker, it is harmful not only to the individual directly injured by it but to the whole community. This definition may be applied also to violations of international law. A violation of international law committed by a State is a crime for which the individual perpetrator is punishable if the act is harmful not only to the State directly injured by it but also to the whole international community. The Advisory Committee of Jurists appointed by the Council of the League of Nations in February, 1920, for the purpose of preparing plans for the establishment of the Permanent Court of International Justice, discussed the question of conferring upon the Court competence in criminal matters. In the course of the discussion, Baron Descamps raised the question, "Do crimes against the Law of Nations exist?" He answered the question in the affirmative by defining these "crimes" as acts "of such a nature that the security of all States would be imperilled by them." * The formula "imperil the security of all States" means about the same as the perhaps better formula "harmful to the international community." The Committee did not clear up the question as to which violations of international law "imperil the security of all States." It seems that Descamps took it for granted that not all violations of international law are "crimes," in the sense of his definition. He considered it necessary to authorize the International Court

* Permanent Court of International Justice, Advisory Committee of Jurists, *Procès verbaux of the Proceedings of the Committee, June 16–July 24, 1920* (The Hague. 1920), p. 498.

"to define the character of the offense," * by which he probably meant that the Court should decide whether the offense
had the character of a "crime" or not. It is, however, hardly
possible to draw a clear line between violations of international law which are harmful to the international community and therefore crimes for which the individual perpetrator may be punished, and violations of international law
which are not of such a nature. Since any violation of law is
harmful to the legal community, the legal order attaches to
any violation a sanction. The only difference that exists concerns the degree to which a delict is harmful to the community. To acts considered more harmful the national legal
order attaches punishments, to acts considered less harmful,
civil execution. A differentiation of the sanction into punishment and civil execution can hardly be introduced into
international law. But, as we shall see later, sanctions which
are to be directed against individuals made responsible for
violations of international law can be much more differentiated than they usually are in national criminal law. It is
not possible by an absolute criterion to distinguish "punishment" from a sanction which has not this character. It is
therefore advisable not to use the term "punishment" in
connection with the problem of individual responsibility
for violations of international law, but individual sanctions, in contradistinction to collective sanctions of general

* *Ibid.,* p. 512. Baron Descamps took his idea from the institution of
ministerial responsibility established by the constitution of his country.
He said (p. 512): "The Belgian Constitution, which is so liberal, and so
scrupulous in its enforcement of penalties, does not hesitate to lay down
that the House of Representatives may bring charges against the Ministers
and bring them to trial before the Court of Cassation, which is expressly
invested with power to define the offence and to determine the punishment." Individual responsibility of the organ of State for a violation of
international law is, indeed, analogous to the individual responsibility of a
member of government for a violation of the constitution or another rule
of national law (impeachment in Great Britain).

international law; or if the term "punishment" is used, it may be advisable to define it as a sanction directed against an individual made responsible for a violation of international law.

With respect to the individual responsibility to be established for violations of international law, we must distinguish violations of international law by acts of State and violations by acts which do not have this character. Among the former, four groups of offenses can be distinguished: (1) by resorting to war in disregard of general or particular international law (Briand-Kellogg Pact, and the like); (2) by provoking war—that is to say, by committing the international delict against which war is a just reaction (the delict of provoking war is of no account if the Covenant establishing the Court permits war only as a collective sanction and if it is executed by or under the authority of the League); (3) by violating the rules of warfare; (4) by violating other norms of general or particular international law.*

The trial of an individual who, in his capacity as an organ of State, is held responsible for his State's violation of international law, may take place in conjunction with the procedure of the court in an action by a State or by an international agency (such as the Council of the League) against a State accused of having committed one of the offenses mentioned *sub* 1-4. After having decided that a State has violated international law, the court may at the request of the injured State, open a procedure against the individual who, as organ of the guilty State, must be held responsible for the latter's violation of the law. In case of offenses men-. tioned *sub* 1 and 2, procedure against the responsible indi-

* In the discussion of the Advisory Committee of Jurists, Lord Phillimore differentiated: 1. Acts committed in time of peace; 2. Crimes of war; 3. The crime of having made war.—*Ibid.*, p. 507.

vidual may be opened also at the request of the international agency.

The punishment inflicted by the court upon the individual held responsible for his State's violation of international law does not prevent the court from imposing upon the guilty State the obligation to repair the wrong done. The penalties to be inflicted upon the guilty individuals should be determined by the court in accordance with the criminal law of the State of the accused. Since, however, the acts mentioned *sub* 1 and 2 do not constitute crimes according to national law, the court may be authorized to inflict upon the guilty individual in case of an offense mentioned *sub* 1 and 2, any penalty which the court thinks to be adequate. Death penalty, however, should be excluded if the criminal law of the accused does not provide this penalty. In case of an offense mentioned *sub* 3 (war crime), the court should inflict upon the accused the penalty which the criminal law of his State would provide for the act if it had not the character of an act of State but were an ordinary crime.

The offenses mentioned *sub* 4, like those *sub* 1 and 2, do not, as a rule, constitute acts which, according to national law, would be crimes if they were not acts of State. In most of these cases, the delict of the organ responsible for his State's violation of international law is much less harmful to the international community than in the cases mentioned *sub* 1 to 3. Consequently, the individual sanctions to be attached to these delicts, if the latter do not constitute crimes according to general criminal law, must be much less severe than those inflicted upon war criminals or the authors of a war. The purpose of the penalty in the case of the offenses mentioned *sub* 4 should be to stigmatize the guilty persons morally and politically rather than to inflict upon them a

physical harm, such as imprisonment, or a fine. Such penalties are: the loss of political rights, the loss of capacity to
hold public office, etc. The Court may even restrict its sentence to the declaration that the accused has violated international law (or is personally responsible for his State's
violation of international law).

Violations of international law by acts of individuals, not
acts of State, are divisible into two groups: (1) Acts which
the States to which the individuals are subject are obligated to punish; to this group belong war crimes committed
not at the command or with the authorization of the government (when the delinquent has fallen into the hands of
the authorities of the injured State, there exists, as a rule,
concurrent jurisdiction of the latter). (2) Acts which the
State to which the individuals are subject is not obliged to
punish but which either all the States or the injured States
are authorized by international law to punish or against
which they are authorized to impose a sanction not having
exactly the character of punishment; to this group belong
such acts as piracy, breach of blockade, carriage of contraband, espionage, war treason, and the like.

If an international court is established competent to decree sanctions not only against States for violations of international law, but also against individuals responsible for
such violations, it is not necessary to confer upon this court,
as to a tribunal of first instance, jurisdiction over individuals accused of having violated international law by
acts which have not the character of acts of State. If their
State, as in the case mentioned *sub* 1, is obliged to punish
them, and if it does not fulfill this obligation, the injured
State is in a position to bring the guilty State and its responsible organ to justice before the international court. It is,
however, possible and advisable to give the injured State

the right of appealing to the international court if the sentence of the national court seems not to be satisfactory. If the delinquent is within the legal power of a third State, member of the League, the State obligated to punish him should be bound to ask for his extradition and the third State obliged to grant it. When the delinquent is sentenced not by a court of his own State but by the court of a foreign State and, in particular, by a court of the injured State, the sentenced individual as well as his State should have a right of appeal to the international court. The substantive law to be applied by the international court must be the law of the court against whose sentence appeal has been made. In the cases mentioned *sub* 2, it is likewise advisable to confer upon the individual sentenced by a national court and, if the accused is a citizen of another member State, upon his own State the right to appeal to the international court. If the national court has applied in its sentence national criminal law, as in the case of piracy, the international court as court of appeal has to apply the same national law. If the national court has decreed a sanction directly determined by international law, as in the case of breach of blockade or carriage of contraband (confiscation of the vessel and the cargo). the international court has to apply international law.

Acts of individuals which are not acts of State, as a rule, are violations of international law, since they are internationally injurious. The term "internationally injurious" means that the act injures a State other than the State which bears vicarious responsibility for it since the act has been committed on its territory, such as, for instance, an insult to the flag of a foreign State. Acts of private individuals for which no State is responsible, such as, for instance, piracy, are internationally injurious insofar as they violate interests

Guaranteed by Individual Responsibility   123

of a State authorized by international law to punish them.
It is possible, however, that an international treaty may
obligate the contracting States to provide punishment for
certain crimes which do not constitute injuries to another
State, but whose punishment is in the common interest of
the contracting States, such as traffic in opium, and the like.
In these cases too, the international court may have jurisdiction as a court of appeal, and the accused as well as each
contracting State may have the right to appeal from the
competent national court to the international court. The
latter may also decide conflicts of competence between national courts.

Any person directly injured by the delict which is the
subject of the judicial procedure may, if authorized by the
court, and subject to any conditions which it may impose,
constitute himself *partie civile* before the court; such person
shall not take part in the oral proceeding except when the
court is dealing with the damages.*

At the request of the international court any State as a
member of the League should be obliged to commit to that
court any individual who is under the jurisdiction and
within the power of the State concerned. The court may
decide whether an individual who has been committed
to it shall be placed under arrest, and under what conditions he may be set at liberty. The State on whose territory
the court is sitting must place at the court's disposal all
means necessary for effective judicial procedure, such as a
suitable place of internment, a staff of wardens for the cus-
tody of persons placed under arrest, and the like.†

* See Article 26 of the Convention for the Creation of an International
Criminal Court, *Proceedings of the International Conference on the Repression of Terrorism*, Series of League of Nations Publications, Legal, 1938,
v. 3, p. 23.
† See Article 31 of the above-quoted Convention, *ibid.*, p. 25.

The orders and sentences of the international court should be executed by the State designated in the order or the sentence of the court. If a State fails to fulfill its obligation to execute an order or sentence of the international court, the collective sanctions provided by the Covenant constituting the League as a judicial community should come into operation.

Annexes

ANNEX I

COVENANT

of a

PERMANENT LEAGUE
FOR THE MAINTENANCE OF PEACE

Article 1

1. Members of the Permanent League for the Maintenance of Peace are the Contracting Parties and those other States as shall accede without reservation to this Covenant. Such accession shall be effected by a declaration deposited with the Secretariat. Notice thereof shall be sent to all other Members of the League.

2. Any doubt as to whether a community which has declared its accession to the League is a State in the sense of international law is settled by a decision of the Court.

Organs of the League

Article 2

The organs of the League are:

       a. The Assembly
       b. The Court
       c. The Council
       d. The Secretariat

THE ASSEMBLY

Article 3

1. The Assembly shall consist of representatives of the Members of the League.

2. The Assembly shall meet at stated intervals and from time to time as occasion may require at the seat of the League or at such other place as may be decided upon.

3. At meetings of the Assembly, each Member of the League shall have one vote and may have not more than one representative.

4. The Government of . . . . shall summon the first meeting of the Assembly. Its representative shall preside over the first session.

5. The representatives on the Assembly shall preside over the following sessions in rotation in alphabetical order in English of the names of the States which they represent. A president shall enter into office at the beginning of the session and remain in office until the opening of the next session.

6. The Assembly is competent to adopt decisions binding upon the Members only in matters provided in this Covenant. Except where otherwise expressly provided in this Covenant, decisions of the Assembly (including elections) require the simple majority of votes of the Members present at the meeting.

7. The Assembly may discuss any matter affecting the international situation and express its opinion by resolutions adopted by a majority of the Members present at the meeting.

8. The Assembly may draw up its rules of procedure.

THE COURT

Article 4

The Court shall consist of 17 members appointed from amongst persons of high moral character who are experts in international law.

Article 5

The members of the Court shall be appointed for life in accordance with the following provisions.

or

Article 4

1. The Court shall consist of 17 members.

2. The members of the Court shall be appointed from amongst persons of high moral character who are experts in international law in accordance with the following provisions: (In this case Article 5 is dropped.)

Article 6

1. Each Government of a State Member of the League shall invite its highest courts of justice, its legal faculties and schools of law, and its national academies and national sections of international academies devoted to the study of law to nominate two persons in a position to accept the duties of a member of the Court.

2. Only one of them shall be of their own nationality. The same person can be nominated by different institutions of the same State as well as by institutions of different States.

3. Each Government shall inscribe the person thus nominated by the institutions of its State in a list and forward this list to the Secretary General of the League.

Article 7

The Secretary General shall prepare a list of all persons thus nominated according to the following provisions:

Article 8

1. The first part of the list shall consist of the persons nominated by institutions which are not of their own nationality.

2. The order in which these persons shall be registered is determined by the number of foreign States the institutions of which have nominated the respective person. A person who is nominated by institutions of more foreign States precedes a person nominated by institutions of fewer foreign States. A person nominated not only by institutions of one or more foreign States, but also by institutions of his own State, precedes persons nominated by the institutions of the same number of foreign States but by no institutions of their own States.

3. Persons nominated by institutions of the same number of States (their own States included) are classed according to the number of institutions by which they have been nominated. In case they have been nominated by the same number of institutions, they shall be registered in alphabetical order.

4. The same principle applies to the persons nominated only by institutions of one foreign State.

Article 9

The second part of the list to be prepared by the Secretary General shall consist of the persons nominated by institutions of their own States. These persons shall be registered in the alphabetical order of the names of their States. Within each national group the persons are classed according to the number of their national institutions by which they have been nominated.

Article 10

1. The first nine persons registered in the first part of the list of experts shall be considered as appointed members of the Court. The other eight members of the Court shall be elected from the second part of the list by the Assembly of the League according to the majority vote principle.

2. For each of the eight seats a separate election shall be arranged. If two (three) ballots do not produce a majority, the nine judges appointed according to Section 1 of this Article shall elect the judge from the second part of the list of experts.

Article 11

Should one of the members of the Court either die or resign or be dismissed by the Court according to Article 17, the Court shall elect a member from that part of the list from which the deceased, resigned, or dismissed member had been selected.

or

Should one of the members of the Court who has been selected from the first part of the list of experts (Art. 8) either die, resign, or be retired or dismissed according to Article 17, the Court shall elect a judge from that part of the list; if he has been selected from the second part of the list (Art. 9), the Assembly shall elect a judge from that part of the list. If two (three) ballots do not produce a majority, the Court shall elect a judge from the second part of the list.

Article 12

The list of experts to be prepared by the Secretary General shall be renewed every fourth year according to the provisions of Articles 6 to 9.

Article 13

The members of the Court are independent.

Article 14

The members of the Court shall enjoy diplomatic privileges and immunities in all the States Members of the League; their citizenship and allegiance to their home States is suspended during their function as members of the Court. The document certifying their membership in the Court shall be recognized as diplomatic passport by all the States Members of the League.

Article 15

1. The members of the Court may not exercise any political or administrative function nor engage in any other occupation of professional nature.

2. Any doubt on this point is settled by the decision of the Court.

Article 16

1. No member of the Court may act as agent, counsel, or advocate in any case.

2. No member may participate in the consideration and decision of any case in which his home State is one of the contesting parties, or in any case in which he has previously taken an active part as agent, counsel, or advocate for one of the contesting parties or as a member of a national or

international court, or of a commission of inquiry, or in any other capacity.

3. Any doubt on this point is settled by the decision of the Court.

Article 17

1. A judge may resign his office.

2. When a judge has become physically or mentally unable to exercise his function, he can be retired by a decision of the Court adopted by the majority of the other members.

or

2. When a judge has finished his seventieth year of age he is obliged to retire (he can be retired by a decision of the Court adopted by the majority of the other members).

3. If a judge ceases to fulfill the conditions required by Article 4, he can be dismissed by a decision of the Court adopted unanimously by the other members.

Article 18

Every member of the Court shall, before taking up his duties, make a solemn declaration in open Court that he will exercise his power impartially and conscientiously.

Article 19

1. The Court shall elect its president and vice-president for three years; they may be re-elected.

2. It shall appoint its registrar.

Article 20

1. The seat of the Court shall be established at the seat of the League.

2. All the members of the Court shall reside at the seat of the Court.

Article 21

The Court shall remain permanent in session except during the judicial vacations, the dates and duration of which shall be fixed by the Court.

Article 22

1. If, for some special reason, a member of the Court considers that he should not take part in the decision of a particular case, he shall so inform the president.

2. If the president considers that for some special reason one of the members of the Court should not sit on a particular case, he shall give him notice accordingly.

3. If in any such case the member of the Court and the president disagree, the matter shall be settled by the decision of the Court.

Article 23

1. The full Court shall sit except when it is expressly provided otherwise.

2. A quorum of eleven judges shall suffice to constitute the full Court.

3. All questions shall be decided by a majority of the judges present at the meeting. In the event of an equality of votes, the president or his deputy shall have a casting vote.

Article 24

1. The Court is authorized to frame rules for regulating its procedure (Rules of Court).

2. The Rules of Court may provide for the establishment of Chambers composed of five (seven) judges and determine the cases on which a Chamber shall sit.

Article 25

The official language of the Court shall be English, but each party may use the language of its country. The Court shall make adequate arrangements for the translation into English of any oral or written declaration directed to the Court in other than the official language.

Article 26

1. The members of the Court shall receive an annual salary.

2. The president shall receive a special annual allowance.

3. The vice-president shall receive a special allowance for every day on which he acts as president.

4. · These salaries and allowances shall be fixed by the Assembly of the League.

THE COUNCIL

Article 27

1. The United States of America, the United Kingdom of Great Britain and Northern Ireland, the Union of Soviet Socialist Republics, and China are permanent members of the Council.

2. Non-permanent members of the Council shall be chosen by the Assembly only for a fixed term.

3. The Assembly shall fix the rules dealing with the election of the non-permanent members of the Council and particularly such regulations as relate to their office and conditions of re-eligibility.

4. At the meetings of the Council each Member of the

League represented on the Council shall have one vote and not more than one representative.

5. The Government of . . . . shall summon the first meeting of the Council; its representative shall preside over the first session.

6. Over the following sessions the representatives on the Council shall preside in rotation in alphabetical order in English of the names of the States which they represent. A president shall enter into office at the beginning of the session and remain in office until the opening of the next session.

7. The Council is competent to adopt decisions binding upon the members only in matters provided for in this Covenant.

8. Except where otherwise expressly provided in this Covenant, decisions of the Council require the simple majority of votes of the members present at the meeting.

9. The Council may draw its rules of procedure.

THE SECRETARIAT

Article 28

1. The Secretariat is established at the seat of the League. The Secretariat shall comprise a Secretary General and such secretaries and staff as may be required.

2. The Secretary General shall be appointed by a decision of the Assembly. He may be removed from office in the same way. He may also resign.

3. The secretaries and staff of the Secretariat shall be appointed by the Secretary General with the approval of the Council.

4. The Secretary General shall act in that capacity at all meetings of the Assembly and of the Council.

Article 29

The expenses of the League shall be borne by the Members of the League in the proportion decided by the Assembly.

SEAT OF THE LEAGUE AND PRIVILEGES OF THE REPRESENTATIVES

Article 30

1. The seat of the League is established at . . . .

2. The Council may at any time decide that the seat of the League shall be established elsewhere.

3. Representatives of the Members of the League and officials of the League when engaged on the business of the League shall enjoy diplomatic privileges and immunities.

4. The buildings and other property occupied by the League or its officials or representatives attending its meetings shall be inviolable.

COMPETENCE OF THE COURT

Article 31

1. If there should arise between Members of the League any dispute, any party to the dispute may submit the matter to the Court.

2. The Court is competent to decide any dispute between Members of the League submitted by one of the parties to the dispute.

Article 32

The Court is competent to decide a dispute between a Member and a State which is not a Member of the League if the latter, by a declaration deposited with the Court, accepts the provisions of Articles 33-36 with the rights and obligations of a Member for the purpose of such dispute.

Article 33

1. In deciding disputes mentioned in Articles 31 and 32, the Court shall apply the rules of International Law.

2. The general principles of law recognized by civilized nations are considered to be part of International Law.

3. The Court shall decide a case *ex aequo et bono* if the parties agree thereto.

PROHIBITION OF WAR AND REPRISALS

Article 34

No member of the League is allowed to resort to war or reprisals against another Member except in cases foreseen in Article 35 and Article 36, Section 2 of this Covenant.

SANCTIONS AGAINST MEMBER STATES

Article 35

Should any Member of the League resort to war or reprisals against another Member of the League in disregard of its obligation under Article 34 the Court shall, on the request of the injured Member or of the Council, decide the question whether the accused Member has violated the Covenant. In accordance with this decision the Council shall order the necessary economic or military sanctions against the Member declared responsible for the violation.

EXECUTION

Article 36

1. All orders and decisions of the Court and the Council must be executed in full good faith by the Member State designated in the order or decision.

2. If a Member State does not fulfill this obligation the Council shall, at the request of the Court or on its own initiative, order the necessary measures destined to assure the execution.

3. In the event the Member State concerned should object to the order or decision to be executed excess of jurisdiction, the matter shall be settled by a decision of the Court.

Article 37

If the Member of the League against which the measures provided for by Articles 35 and 36 are directed is a member of the Council, its representative shall be excluded from the consideration and decision in this matter.

ANNULMENT OF TREATIES

Article 38

The Assembly may, by a two-thirds majority, declare inapplicable treaties to which only Members of the League are parties if it considers such treaties not to be adapted to existing international conditions. A treaty declared inapplicable becomes invalid six months after this declaration.

AMENDMENTS

Article 39

1. Amendments to the present Covenant will take effect when voted by the Assembly on a three-fourth majority (in

which there shall be included the votes of all the members of the Council represented at the meeting).

2. Amendments concerning only the number of judges composing the Court shall take effect when voted by the Assembly on a simple majority.

3. The text of the present Covenant, the amendments subsequently adopted, and the decisions of the Court shall be published in an Official Journal by the Secretary General. The text of the Covenant and its amendments thus published is authentic.

RATIFICATION

Article 40

The present Covenant shall enter into force when ratified by the United States of America, the United Kingdom of Great Britain and Northern Ireland, the Union of Soviet Socialistic Republics, China, and ten other signatories.

ANNEX II

———

TREATY STIPULATIONS ESTABLISHING INDIVIDUAL
RESPONSIBILITY FOR VIOLATIONS OF INTERNATIONAL
LAW (INTERNATIONAL CRIMINAL JURISDICTION).

*Articles 4, 6, 7, 8, 9, 10, 11, 12, and 24 of the Covenant in
Annex I may be replaced or modified by the following stipulations:*

Article 4

The Court shall consist of twenty-four (17) members
appointed from amongst persons of high moral character.
Seventeen (12) members shall be experts in international
law, seven (5) members experts in criminal law.

Article 5
unchanged
or
Article 4

1. The Court shall consist of twenty-four (17) members,
seventeen (12) members being experts in international law,
seven (5) members experts in criminal law.

2. The members of the Court shall be appointed from
amongst persons of high moral character in accordance with
the following provisions: (In this case Article 5 is dropped.)

Article 6

1. . . . . to nominate two experts in international
law and two experts in criminal law, in a position . . . .

141

2. Only one of the two in each group shall be . . . .

3. . . . . in two lists, one comprising the persons nominated as experts in international law, the other comprising the persons nominated as experts in criminal law. Both lists shall be forwarded to the . . . .

Article 7

. . . . two lists of the persons thus nominated, one comprising all experts in international law, the other comprising all experts in criminal law, according to . . . .

Article 8

1. The first part of each list shall . . . .
2. Unchanged
3. Unchanged
4. Unchanged

Article 9

The second part of each list to be . . . .

Article 10

1. The first nine (6) persons registered in the first part of the list of experts in international law and the first four (3) persons registered in the first part of the list of experts in criminal law shall be considered as appointed members of the Court. The other eight (6) members experts in international law and the other three (2) members experts in criminal law shall be elected from the second part of the respective list of experts by the . . . .

2. For each of the eight (6) members experts in international law and the three (2) members experts in criminal law a separate election shall be arranged. If in the election of one of the eight (6) members experts in international

law two (3) ballots do not produce a majority, the nine (6) judges experts in international law appointed according to Section 1 of this Article shall elect the judge from the second part of the list of experts in international law. If in the election of one of the three (2) members experts in criminal law two (3) ballots do not produce a majority, the four (3) judges experts in criminal law appointed according to Section 1 of this article, shall elect the judge from the second part of the list of experts in criminal law.

Article 11

. . . . from that part of the respective list from which . . . .

or

Should one of the members of the Court who has been selected from the first part of one of the two lists of experts (Art. 8) either die, ..., the Court shall elect a judge from that part of the respective list; if he has been selected from the second part of one of the two lists (Art. 9) the Assembly shall elect a judge from that part of the respective list. If two (3) ballots do not produce a majority, the Court shall elect the judge from the second part of the respective list of experts.

Article 12

The two lists of experts to be prepared . . . .

Article 24

1. Unchanged
2. Unchanged
3. In each Chamber one part of the judges must be experts in international law, the other part experts in criminal law.

The following Articles may be inserted between Articles 35 and 36 of the Covenant in Annex I:

COMPETENCE OF THE COURT AS CRIMINAL COURT
OF FIRST (AND LAST) INSTANCE

Article 35 a

1. After the sanction ordered by the Council according to Article 35 has been carried out, the Court shall, at the request of the injured Member State or of the Council, ascertain the individuals who as organs of the guilty State are responsible for the latter's violation of the Covenant.

2. The Court is authorized to sentence the guilty individuals to penalties which it thinks to be adequate. Death penalty, however, is excluded if the law of the State whose organ has been found guilty does not provide such penalty.

Article 35 b

1. Any violation of the laws of warfare committed by a member of the Government of a Member State, or at the command, or with the authorization of such Government, may be brought to justice before the Court at the request of the injured Member State or the Council.

2. The Court is authorized to sentence the guilty individual to the penalty which the criminal law of the State whose organ is responsible for the war crime provides for the act if the latter were not an act of State. If that law does not provide a penalty for such an act, the Court shall fix the penalty according to its discretion.

Article 35 c

If the State whose organs shall be brought to justice before the Court is a member of the Council, its representative shall be excluded from the consideration and decision in the matter of the request to be made by the Council according to Article 35 a, Section 1, and Article 35 b, Section 1.

Article 35 d

1. After having decided the dispute referred to in Articles 31 and 32, the Court shall, at the request of the State which according to the decision of the Court has been injured by the other State, ascertain the individuals who as organs of the latter are responsible for its violation of international law.

2. The Court is authorized to inflict upon the guilty persons as punishment:

    a.   Forfeiture of office
    b.   Forfeiture of capacity to hold public office
    c.   Forfeiture of all political rights

3. Forfeiture of capacity to hold public office or of political rights may be inflicted for a certain period of time or forever.

4. In cases of minor infringements of international law the Court may limit its sentence to the establishment of the fact that the accused is responsible for the violation of international law committed by his State.

COMPETENCE OF THE COURT AS CRIMINAL COURT OF APPEAL

Article 35 e

1. The Court has jurisdiction as a court of appeal in all cases which have been decided by the national court of a Member State and in which an individual has been tried

for having violated international law, or national law the purpose of which is to enforce international law.

2. The following have a right to appeal to the Court:

a. The individual sentenced by the national court;

b. Any Member State injured by the delict for which the individual has been tried;

c. If no State is directly injured by the delict, any State in relation to which the State having exercised jurisdiction is obliged to prosecute the delinquent;

d. If the individual is sentenced by a court which is not a court of his home State, the latter State;

e. The Council of the League.

3. If the State against whose court the Council intends to enact an appeal is a member of the Council, its representative shall be excluded from the consideration and decision in this matter.

Article 35 f

If the sanction to be inflicted upon the delinquent by the national court in the cases referred to in Article 35 e is determined only by national law, the Court has to apply in its decision the law to be applied by the national court. If the sanction is directly determined by international law, the Court has to apply in its decision international law.

EXTRADITION

Article 35 g

When a Member State is internationally obliged to prosecute a crime and when the supposed delinquent is in the territory of another Member State, the latter is obliged, at the request of the former, to extradite the individual concerned provided that the generally recognized conditions of extradition are fulfilled.

PARTIE CIVILE

Article 35 h

Any person directly injured by the delict which is the subject of the judicial procedure referred to in Articles 35 a to 35 d may, if authorized by the Court, and subject to any condition which it may impose, constitute himself *partie civile* before the Court; such person shall not take part in the oral proceeding except when the Court is dealing with the damages.

COMMITMENT OF INDIVIDUALS TO THE COURT

Article 35 i

1. At the request of the Court any Member State is obliged to commit to the Court any individual who is under the jurisdiction and within the power of the State concerned.

2. The Court may decide whether an individual who has been committed to it shall be placed under arrest, and under what conditions he may be set at liberty.

OBLIGATIONS OF THE STATE ON WHOSE TERRITORY THE COURT IS SITTING

Article 35 j

The State on whose territory the Court is sitting is obliged to place at the Court's disposal all facilities necessary for effective judicial procedure.

RIGHT OF PARDON

Article 35 k

1. The right of pardon shall be exercised by the Council of the League.

2. If the person who has been sentenced by the Court according to Article 35 a or 35 b is the organ of a State which is a member of the Council, or if the person who has been sentenced by the Court according to Article 35 e has been tried in the first instance by the court of a State which is a member of the Council, the representative of this State shall be excluded from the consideration and decision in the matter of pardon.

INDEX

ABSOLUTE liability, 73

Act of State, responsibility for, 79, 81ff., 96ff.; performed at superior command and act of State, difference between, 104; of government, nullity or annullability of, 106

Administrative agency, international, 20; as auxiliary organ of an international court, 20

Aggression, protection against, 51f., 65; external, and internal peace, 52ff., 55

Amendments to Covenant of P.L.M.P., 64, 139

Anarchism, 3

Anarchy, international, 17

Annulment of treaties, 139

Application and creation of law no absolute antagonism, 47

Arbitration, treaties, effectiveness of, 21; tribunals, in primitive law, 21f

Armament, restriction of, 51

Assembly of P.L.M.P., 128

Authors of war, individual responsibility of, 71ff.

Autonomy, equality as identical with, 37f.; of the States limited by international law, 39

BASIC Field Manual, Rules of Land Warfare, 105

Bellum justum (just war), 71f., 89f., 95

Blockade, breach of, 76f.

Blood revenge, 4

Briand-Kellogg Pact, 18, 44, 65, 71, 91, 95

CAUSES of war, 16f.

Central American Court of Justice, 49

Centralization, of use of force, 4, 19; advantages of, 10; usual degree of, in international communities, 12f., 19, 40f., 42, 51; world organization a problem of, 21; law-applying preceding law-creating function, 21f.; of executive power and federal state, 51, 55

Clausula rebus sic stantibus, 30

Collective responsibility, and individual responsibility in international law, 71ff.; established by general international law, 74f.

Commitment of individuals to court of P.L.M.P., 147

Conflicts of competence decided by international court, 123

Compulsory adjudication of international disputes and sovereign equality of States, 34ff., 44ff., 47f.

Compulsory jurisdiction, 14ff.

Conciliation, 31, 32ff., 63

Confederacy of States or World State, 9ff.

Contract, social, 6f., 9

Convention for Protection of

149

Index 155

Territorial integrity of members of an international community, 52f.

Treaty, international imposing duties upon third States, 28; relating to use of submarines, 78f.; of Washington, 78f.; for protection of submarine telegraph cables, 79f.; of Versailles, 88ff., 109, 112; on prisoners of war, 108f., 112

Tribunals, in primitive law, 21f.; international, majority vote principle, 43; applying positive international law, 44; applying pre-existing law, 46f.

UNANIMOUS vote principle in international relations, 37, 42

United States as model of world State, 11f.

VERSAILLES, treaty of, 88ff., 109f., 112

Vicarious responsibility of State, 78

Violation of international law by private persons, 78, 122f.

Void *ab initio* or voidable, 105f.

WAR, as employment of force, 5; renunciation of, 14ff., 18; causes of, 16f.; as sanction of international law, 18, 53f., 74f.

War crimes, 77f., 91ff.; as violations of international or national law, 101ff.

War criminals, punishment of, 72, 91ff., 109ff., 114f.

War guilt in first and second World War, 88ff.

War treason, individual responsibility for, 99f.

Warfare, illegitimate acts of, 77f., 95; rules of, violation of, 92ff.; legitimate acts of, 93ff.

World government, 5, 13, 50

World organization, 5f., 9ff.; a problem of centralization, 21

World parliament, 5, 10, 13, 50

World peace, 5f.

World State, 5f., 9ff.

www.ingramcontent.com/pod-product-compliance
Lightning Source LLC
Chambersburg PA
CBHW020813300326
41914CB00075B/1739/J